So you *really* want to learn

History

Britain 1066-1500

Answer Book

CHILTON CANTELO SCHOOL
YEOVIL, SOMERSET

Name	Form	Issued	Returned

So you <u>really</u> want to learn

History

Britain 1066-1500

Answer Book

Bob Pace M.A.

Series Editor: Niall Murphy M.A. (Cantab)

CHILTON CANTELO

GALORE PARK

www.galorepark.co.uk

Published by Galore Park Publishing Ltd
19/21 Sayers Lane, Tenterden, Kent TN30 6BW

www.galorepark.co.uk

Typography by Typetechnique, London W1
Illustration by Jane Humphrey

Printed and bound by CPI Antony Rowe, Chippenham

ISBN-13: 978 1 90573 506 8

First published 2008, reprinted 2009

Details of other Galore Park publications are available at www.galorepark.co.uk

ISEB Revision Guides, publications and examination papers may also be obtained from Galore Park.

Contents

Introduction

The purpose of this answer book is to assist teachers and parents to assess the answers to the questions in *So you really want to learn History Book One: Britain 1066-1500*. These answers, therefore, are not absolutely hard and fast.

So you really want to learn History Book One: Britain 1066-1500 provides a wide variety of written tasks from simple fill-in-the-blank exercises to full Common Entrance-style essays. The simpler exercises can be more exactly answered and a mark scheme is provided to help teachers. However, with the essay questions it is frankly impossible to provide a definitive answer. What is provided is guidance to help teach pupils the skills needed to be successful in both analysing sources and writing descriptive and explanatory essays. In the marking of the evidence questions and essays the Common Entrance marking scheme (reproduced here as an appendix) needs to be consulted alongside the comments given alongside each answer. Developing skills to deal with these tasks should, in the short term, help pupils to do well in the Common Entrance examination and, in the longer term, help them to develop a more mature and thoughtful approach to their work and to the world of information around them.

Bob Pace
March 2008

Chapter 1 The Norman Conquest

Exercise 1.1

1. *Edward the Confessor died in January 1066.*

2. *Edgar the Atheling was considered too young to become king.*

3. *The English army at this time was made up of elite troops called housecarls and lesser soldiers known as the fyrd.*

4. *William of Normandy had to convince his barons to support him before he could plan his invasion of England.*

5. *Harald Hardrada and Tostig were defeated at the Battle of Stamford Bridge.*

6. *William of Normandy set up his castle at Hastings to wait for King Harold.*

7. *The English army under King Harold set up their shieldwall on Senlac Hill.*

8. *The Normans had knights, which the English did not have.*

9. *King Harold's two brothers, Gyrth and Leofwine, were killed in the Battle of Hastings.*

10. *The Bayeux Tapestry appears to show King Harold being hit in the eye with an arrow, though he might also be the figure being cut down by a Norman knight.*

Total for exercise: 10 marks

Exercise 1.2

Pupils need to identify Harald Hardrada, Harold Godwinson and William of Normandy as the three claimants, together with a summary of their respective claims.

Harald Hardrada – *Hardrada based his claim on an earlier agreement between the kings of England and Norway over who should be king if there was no heir. He argued that his predecessor Magnus should have become King of England, whom he should have succeeded.*

Harold Godwinson – *Harold claimed that Edward the Confessor, on his death-bed, had named him as his successor. This was approved by the Witan. Harold was the most powerful earl in England and Edward's brother-in-law.*

William of Normandy – *William claimed that Edward had promised him the throne in 1052. Furthermore, in 1064 Harold had sworn a sacred oath to confirm this. William was a distant cousin of Edward, whose mother was Norman.*

Total for exercise: 6 marks

Exercise 1.3

2.	Edward promises the throne to William.	(g)	1052
8.	Harold swears fealty to William.	(f)	1064
7.	Edward dies.	(e)	5th January 1066
4.	Harold is crowned.	(a)	6th January 1066
3.	Halley's comet seen.	(d)	April 1066
10.	Battle of Fulford.	(b)	20th September 1066
1.	Battle of Stamford Bridge.	(i)	25th September 1066
9.	The Normans land at Pevensey.	(c)	28th September 1066
5.	The armies take up position on Senlac Hill.	(j)	13th October 1066
6.	Battle of Hastings.	(h)	14th October 1066

Total for exercise: 10 marks

Exercise 1.4

1. Source A gives three reasons to choose from: Harold was taken by surprise; Harold and his brothers were killed; and God granted the victory to the Normans because of the sins of the English. The pupil may choose any of these, and a good answer should use a quotation from the source.

    The source suggests that Harold was unprepared for the Norman attack: 'And William came against him by surprise'. (2 marks)

2. A good answer should mention most of the following reasons: the Norman 'feigned flight'; the large number of deaths on the English side; the cramped fighting conditions; the deaths of Harold and his brothers; and the eventual retreat of the English. Quotations should be used.

    The source states that the English lost because of the Normans' trick of pretending to retreat: 'Twice this trick was used successfully'. Also because the English had lost so many men, including the important figures of King Harold, Leofwine and Gyrth: 'They had lost most of their army, the King and two of his brothers were dead'. (3 marks)

3. This answer should mention the points that Source A makes, which Source B does not, and vice versa. Those exclusive to Source A include the English being surprised, and the

eventual Norman victory being due to the sins of the English. Source B mentions the Norman 'feigned flights' and the cramped fighting conditions, which Source A does not. A more careful answer might also mention in passing that the two sources agree on a number of factors. Accurate use of quotations should be rewarded.

The two sources disagree in several respects as to why the English lost. Source A talks about the English being unprepared: 'William came against him by surprise'. This is not mentioned in Source B. Source B talks about the trick retreats: 'Twice this trick was used successfully', not mentioned in Source A. Source A talks about the Normans winning because 'God granted it to them', whilst Source B doesn't mention this at all. However, the two sources do agree on the loss of Harold and the deaths of his two brothers as being very important to the English defeat. (7 marks)

4. A good answer here should point out that Source A is an English source while Source B is written by a Norman. It should also be noted that neither source gives information about when the source was produced and if either of the two authors was an eyewitness (as it happens, neither was). Any evidence of bias should be quoted, though this is difficult to identify in these extracts.

    It is hard to trust totally either of these two sources because Source B was written by a Norman who worked for William and would naturally support his cause. Source A was written by an English monk and we don't know how much he saw or if he was even at the battle, whilst William of Poitiers might have been as we know he was a soldier. However, a monk might have been able to get a good all-round knowledge of an event from the visitors that passed through his monastery. Also we do not know how soon after the battle each author was writing; if it was a long time then there may be inaccuracies. Both sources are trying to explain their point of view, so William of Poitiers is bound to be pro-Norman, whereas the Anglo-Saxon Chronicle is bound to favour the English. (8 marks)

    Total for exercise: 20 marks

Exercise 1.5

1. (a) The list should include most of the following reasons: *Harold and his army were tired after marching south soon after the Battle of Stamford Bridge; William's army was well rested; William showed real leadership during the battle; some of Harold's fyrd were ill-disciplined; William's tactics were better (e.g. the pretend retreats); Harold had not waited for more reinforcements.* The order in which they are placed is less important than the pupil's own explanation of that order: see part (b). (5 marks)

(b) This answer needs to show some understanding of long- and short-term causes. Pupils should show that the events most immediate to the battle, such as Harold not waiting for stronger reinforcements and the Norman army being rested, were themselves dictated by earlier events, i.e. the forced march south from Stamford Bridge. The following is a sample answer, based on one interpretation of the importance of each cause.

There are a number of reasons why William won and Harold lost the Battle of Hastings. The most important reason is that while William had time to prepare his army for battle and work out his tactics, Harold had made a rushed journey south directly after the Battle of Stamford Bridge, when his army was already tired. This is an important reason for the outcome because if this had not happened, Harold might have been able to wait for reinforcements and he would have been waiting for William, rather than the other way around. This had an effect on the way each army acted during the battle. The English fyrd were ill-disciplined and it is possible that, if Harold had had time to wait for stronger reinforcements, he could have controlled his army better and his army would not have reacted to the Norman pretend retreats. (10 marks)

2. (a) This answer needs to be a narrative, showing the chronological understanding of events. The following is a sample answer, taking the example of William:

William played a key role in the Battle of Hastings and victory was largely due to his actions.

William's actions before the battle were very important. He spent the year carefully preparing for the invasion of England, waiting until the autumn rather than rushing into battle straight away. He gained the Pope's support and also made his barons support his invasion plans. He took time to recruit a strong army which was disciplined and well-fed, and built a huge fleet of ships. Although his crossing was delayed slightly by bad weather, this worked in William's favour because, when he landed on 28th September, Harold was still in Yorkshire having fought at Stamford Bridge. William could therefore plunder the countryside and gather supplies while he waited for Harold to appear.

During the battle on 14th October, William's actions made a real difference. In the early stages, his army seemed to be making no headway, but William was persistent. At one point the Bretons on the left flank retreated, causing the English fyrd to run down the hill after them. William was able to think quickly and re-form his soldiers, killing the English fyrd as they broke ranks. He boosted morale by taking off his helmet and rallying his troops personally. It is possible that William commanded his army to keep pretending to retreat, thus luring more English down the hill, though we cannot know this for certain. The

Normans succeeded in killing Harold's brothers, and then, in the final attack, the king himself. With this, the English army fled.

Taking the example of Harold:

Harold Godwinson obviously played a key role in the Battle of Hastings, and his defeat meant the defeat of the English overall.

Harold became king after Edward the Confessor's death, and was recognised by the Witan. He knew that he had rivals to the throne, and spent the spring and summer preparing to fight off Harald Hardrada and William of Normandy. He appointed Edwin and Morcar to defend the north, but struggled to keep his army in place when harvest-time approached. Harald Hardrada and Tostig then defeated Edwin and Morcar at Fulford, so Harold rushed north to defeat the Viking army at Stamford Bridge on 25th September. Now Harold made a big mistake – he rushed south to fight William of Normandy whilst his army was still tired.

At the start of the battle Harold's housecarls stood firm against the Normans but he knew that his local fyrd was inexperienced. Harold kept his army on top of Senlac Hill, and the Norman attacks failed. Then, when the Bretons seemed to fall back, Harold lost control of his army – they ran down the hill and broke the shieldwall formation. Harold and his two brothers were later killed and the battle was lost. (20 marks)

(b) This answer should not be a narrative, but instead should clearly look at success or failure. The best answers will attempt to look at both sides before making a judgement. Taking William as an example:

William had mostly success during the Battle of Hastings but there were also failures.

On the one hand, William experienced failure during the battle. His archers made little impact against the English shieldwall, and the attacks of his foot soldiers and knights made no headway. The retreat of the Bretons was not planned and it nearly became a rout.

On the other hand, William was successful in that his army managed to defeat the English army. William's army was disciplined and well-trained. Considering they had to charge uphill at the English, the Normans did pretty well in wearing down the English army. William also had personal success in turning the retreat of the Bretons into a cunning trick and keeping his army's morale high.

Overall, William's firm leadership and rallying of his troops at the crucial moment meant that he won the Battle of Hastings.

Taking Harold as an example:

Harold had both success and failure during the Battle of Hastings.

On the one hand, he had some success in that his defence was good and initially held up to the Norman attacks. The English fyrd were ill-disciplined but strong, and the shieldwall was an effective barrier. They also had the tactical advantage of being on higher ground.

On the other hand, Harold was a greater failure because of a combination of bad luck and judgement. He was still at Stamford Bridge when William landed on 28th September. This meant that he had to march south an already-tired army. He did not wait to rest his soldiers or to recruit reinforcements but engaged William in battle straight away. During the battle, he relied on the fyrd to keep their positions in the shieldwall. However, when the Bretons retreated, he was unable to stop the fyrd from breaking ranks and running down the hill after them. This weakness in his leadership was a critical mistake and probably cost Harold many of his best men.

Overall, Harold lost the Battle of Hastings because of his haste in wanting to fight William, his lack of leadership in battle, and his bad luck in the timing of the invasion. (10 marks)

3.   (a)   This question should clearly compare and contrast the two opposing sides at either Stamford Bridge or Hastings. Below is an answer comparing the English and Norman soldiers at Hastings.

There were a number of different types of soldiers who fought at Hastings, and the way in which they were equipped and trained made a difference at the battle.

The English army had several different kinds of soldiers who were armed and trained in different ways. The elite troops were called housecarls. These were made up of nobles, the richest and most powerful men in England. They fought with the two-handed axe and were renowned as great fighters. However, the main bulk of the army was the fyrd, poorer men who were recruited from places local to the battle. These men were not as well trained but there were many more of them. They fought with axes, but the tactic used by Harold was to line them up in a wall, bearing their shields. The men at the front of the shieldwall would be well equipped with ringmail armour, metal helmets and strong shields.

The Norman army was also made up of a number of different kinds of soldiers. In fact they were not all Normans: at Hastings, William used Breton soldiers on his left flank and Flemish soldiers on his right. Archers were placed at the front, to fire into the English line, with footsoldiers behind them to charge up the hill. These were armed with swords and long shields. At the rear were knights, who fought on horseback with lances, but also carried swords and sometimes axes. (20 marks)

(b) This answer needs to look at a battle with close reference to the strength and weaknesses of each army.

There are a number of reasons why the Norman army won the Battle of Hastings.

In the days before the battle the Normans had an advantage because they arrived in England with time to prepare, finding food and foraging for supplies. Meanwhile, the English army were at a disadvantage because they were still in the north, and had to quickly re-form. The English were exhausted both by fighting in the Battle of Stamford Bridge and the forced march south. Harold did not wait to recruit reinforcements and, instead, had to use a combination of his tired men and some poorly trained and equipped fyrd he hurriedly gathered.

During the battle the Normans fought well because they were well-equipped, well-disciplined and had an effective military leader in William. Initially, the Norman army faced setbacks because the English shieldwall could not be broken. However, they persevered and succeeded in drawing the less well-disciplined English away from their defensive position, encouraging them to fight. In this situation the Normans were at a great advantage. The English failed at the battle because they allowed themselves to break ranks, and Harold was not able to re-form his men.

Of all the reasons why the Norman army won the Battle of Hastings, the most important was the collapse of the English shieldwall. The strength of the shieldwall was the greatest advantage that the English had. Once it was broken, the English could not recover as the Normans were better equipped and trained, and showed themselves to be superior in hand-to-hand fighting. (10 marks)

Total for exercise: 75 marks

Chapter 2 Conquered England

Exercise 2.1

William I used a number of different methods to control England. He used the *Feudal* System, where the king gave land to *Tenants-in-Chief* in exchange for *soldiers* to fight wars or rebellions.

When a rebellion broke out in the north of England, William punished the people there by the *Harrying* of the *North*. The English made a hero of one rebel, *Hereward the Wake*.

The Normans worked to hold on to their conquered land by building *castles*. The most common type at first was the *motte* and *bailey*. They also rebuilt many of the English *cathedrals*.

In 1085 William ordered a survey of the land to be taken, the results of which were recorded in the *Domesday* Book, to find out, among other things, how much *tax* he should be paid.

Total for exercise: 15 marks

Exercise 2.2

1. *The Feudal System was a system whereby the king gave land to his tenants-in-chief, who in return promised their loyalty to the king. Each tenant-in-chief then gave a portion of his land to those below him, who in turn promised their loyalty.* (2 marks)

2. *Tenants-in-chief were the most important landholders who held their land directly from the king. They were the most powerful barons and churchmen, and controlled the people who lived on their land.* (2 marks)

3. *Homage was the service someone paid to a lord by promising to become his vassal. This included the swearing of fealty, a promise of loyalty, and the obligation to give military service.* (2 marks)

4. *Hereward the Wake was an English rebel who was based in East Anglia and repeatedly fought against the Normans. He became an English hero and a legendary figure.* (2 marks)

5. *In 1069 the English in the north attempted a rebellion with the help of a force of Vikings and Scots, and killed the Norman soldiers in York. William ordered his army to march across Yorkshire laying waste to everything in its path. This became known as the Harrying of the North.* (2 marks)

6. *Motte and bailey castles were buildings that could be built cheaply and quickly. The motte was a mound of earth with a wooden fortified building on top where the soldiers would be based. This*

was surrounded by an enclosure called the bailey, inside which the people, including the baron and his family would live. (2 marks)

7. The new Norman bishops rebuilt churches in the Norman style. These buildings had thick walls with small windows, and were typically decorated with rounded arches. (2 marks)

8. The Domesday Book was compiled in 1085–6. William ordered it to be made because he wanted to know how much money he could raise in taxes, how many men could be expected to provide military service in times of war, and whether his barons were holding land that should be held by him or the Church. The compilers visited every manor and their results were sent to Winchester where the book was written. (2 marks)

Total for exercise: 16 marks

Exercise 2.3

The *manor* was the unit of farming in much of England. Each was held by a *lord*. Most of the people who lived there were *peasants*, or simple farmers. Most would live in a small house that was *timber*-framed and raise vegetables in their *croft*. The main crops were grown in the *open fields*, which were divided into strips. The lord of the manor's land was called the *demesne*.

Total for exercise: 7 marks

Exercise 2.4

woods

church

manor house

croft

peasant's house

common land

Total for exercise: 6 marks

Exercise 2.5

A well-written paragraph should clearly state the sex and status of the chosen peasant. Some understanding of the seasonal nature of the work being done is also important. The best answers will link the type of peasant very clearly to the type of seasonal labour he or she is doing.

> *As the wife of a villein my life is always busy, particularly in the late summer and early autumn. Not only am I busy cooking and looking after the children but I also need to join my husband in the field to harvest the corn, for without this we will starve over the winter. This is made even harder because my husband has to work several days each week on our lord's land, leaving less time to work on our own crops. During the winter I will have clothes to repair and wool to spin, as well as my usual cooking and cleaning. When spring comes my husband will take the plough while I and my daughters follow behind, sowing the seeds and breaking up the rough soil.*

Total for exercise: 10 marks

Exercise 2.6

(a) *Carting dung; threshing corn; digging; spreading manure; and making a ditch.* (2 marks)

(b) A good answer will pick out that the peasant is not rich but always pays his debts on time, helps those poorer than himself, and tries hard not to accept the charity of others. This should be supported by a clear use of quotations from the source.

> *As a peasant, this man cannot be rich, however he gives money to the poor without accepting it himself ('he would help the poor/For the love of Christ and never take a penny') and always pays money when he owes it.* (3 marks)

(c) This answer should describe the two characters with close reference to the source.

> *The people working in the field are 'a poor man hanging on to a plough' and his wife. The man is guiding the plough, which is being pulled by four heifers. His wife is encouraging the oxen with a goad.* (4 marks)

(d) This answer should clearly point out the wretched state of both the man's and woman's clothing, using accurate quotations in support.

> *Langland shows that they are poor by describing their ragged appearance: 'his hood was full of holes', 'his hose hung about his legs on all sides', 'his toes stuck out of his worn shoes'. As for the peasant's wife, 'she walked barefoot on the ice, so that the blood flowed'. This shows that these peasants are too poor to afford new clothes that fit them.* (4 marks)

(e) A good answer will clearly compare the two sources on several points, such as the animals pulling the plough and the person holding a whip. A perceptive answer will also spot that the clothing of the figures in the Luttrell Psalter are not in the poor shape written of in Source B, showing that this is one point where the Psalter differs from Langland. Also a note on the (lack of) relevance of Source A could be included.

The Luttrell Psalter shows two peasants ploughing. One is guiding the plough and another is whipping the oxen. This matches the description of ploughing given by William Langland in Source B, especially when B talks about a 'long goad'. However Langland describes his peasants' appearance as ragged and muddy, with thin-looking oxen. In the Luttrell Psalter the peasants don't seem to have poor clothing, and the oxen look healthy. Geoffrey Chaucer's description of a ploughman in Source A has little to compare with the Luttrell Psalter, since it does not describe the appearance of the peasant, and only mentions types of work (thrashing corn, digging, spreading manure and making a ditch) that are not shown in this part of the Psalter. (7 marks)

Total for exercise: 20 marks

Exercise 2.7

The table below shows a number of suggested entries. It is not exclusive and marks should be awarded for any reasonable suggestion that can be supported. This exercise could initiate a discussion over the nature of kingship: is a successful monarch necessarily a kind, generous individual, or should he or she be cruel and ruthless?

Good points	Bad points
Impressive military ability (Battle of Hastings and Conquest)	Ruthless to those who opposed him (Harrying of the North)
Wise man	Stern and violent rule (burning London at coronation)
Strong and powerful king (use of the Feudal System)	Widespread oppression and distress
Kind to those who loved God (rebuilding of churches)	Greedy (raised taxes; took from the poor)
A good law-maker; kept order (as shown in Domesday Book)	Cruel (ordered poachers to be blinded)

Total for exercise: 10 marks

Chapter 3 The sons of William I

Exercise 3.1

William I left three sons when he died, *Robert, William* and *Henry*. Only *Robert* was never to rule England. William II was very successful at crushing *rebellions* and managed to rule *Normandy* when his brother Robert went on *crusade*. However, William II quarrelled with Archbishop *Anselm* and was killed while hunting in the *New Forest*.

Henry I sorted out the problem of Normandy by capturing and locking *Robert* up. He made peace with Anselm, but they later *quarrelled* over who should choose *bishops* and abbots. However, he encouraged the building of *monasteries*. Henry's biggest problem was who would follow him when his *son* drowned. His daughter, *Matilda*, was next in line.

Total for exercise: 15 marks

Exercise 3.2

1. *William II (1087–1100) was a strong king who crushed rebellions and managed to rule over both England and Normandy. However, he had a terrible temper and didn't seem to care at all about the Church. He was killed while hunting in the New Forest, though nobody knows whether this was accidental or deliberate.* (2 marks)

2. *Archbishop Anselm quarrelled with William II over whether the king or the Pope was in charge of the Church in England. This eventually led to Anselm's exile in 1097. He was reinstated as Archbishop under Henry I, though the argument continued with the new king.* (2 marks)

3. *Robert, Duke of Normandy, was the eldest son of William the Conqueror. He rebelled unsuccessfully against his brother William Rufus and went on the First Crusade. On his return he also rebelled against his brother Henry, who succeeded William Rufus as King of England, and was imprisoned for the rest of his life.* (2 marks)

4. *The White Ship was a vessel which sank in 1120, drowning the son of Henry I. This had serious consequences because it left only Henry's daughter Matilda as his heir.* (2 marks)

5. *Roger, Bishop of Salisbury was appointed to be Henry I's most important official. Henry used Roger's position to support his claim that the king, rather than the Pope, should appoint bishops. Henry argued that bishops were not just Church leaders but could also be major landholders and government officials.* (2 marks)

6. *After 1120 Matilda was Henry I's only surviving legitimate child. She married the Holy Roman Emperor, was widowed and then married Geoffrey Plantagenet. She was Henry's choice to*

succeed him as monarch, despite the opposition of the barons who did not want a woman on the throne. (2 marks)

7. Geoffrey Plantagenet was Matilda's second husband, who later became ruler of Anjou. He was not loyal to Matilda or Henry I, and the king died in 1135 while fighting against him in France. (2 marks)

Total for exercise: 14 marks

Exercise 3.3

1. The table below shows a number of suggested entries. Pupils should pay close attention to the qualities of a 'good king' on page 35 of the textbook. It is common for William II to be dismissed as a wholly 'bad' king. Pupils should avoid this and be encouraged to seek a balanced picture.

William II

Successful	Unsuccessful
Strong military leader (crushed rebellions)	Did not care about the Church (quarrel with Anselm)
Ruled Normandy as well as England	Bad-tempered
	Left no son to succeed him (6 marks)

2. As with question 1 the table below shows some suggested entries.

Henry I

Successful	Unsuccessful
Had some military successes (crushed rebellions)	Not a great warrior himself
Supported the Church in some ways (growth of monasteries)	Argued with the Church in other ways (appointment of bishops)
Encouraged the spread of the justice system in England	Was capable of cruelty
Promoted education and learning	Left no son to succeed him (6 marks)

3. In this answer pupils can make good use of the two lists they have produced.
A suggested answer follows:

I think that Henry I was the better king.

Both kings were successful in some ways. William II was a good military leader, who managed to rule over Normandy as well as England. He also avoided conflict with his brother Robert. Henry I was successful in spreading the justice system in England and promoting education. He was also good in patching up the dispute with Anselm and appointing Roger of Salisbury.

However, both kings had their failures. William II was not very good at upholding the Church and had a terrible temper. Henry I was poor at fighting and could be cruel.

Although both kings had successes and failures, I believe that the more successful was Henry I. This is because the good things that he did, such as spreading the justice system and promoting education, lasted for a long time and were important to the future of England. William II did not have as many successes or good points. (8 marks)

Total for exercise: 20 marks

Exercise 3.4

In a medieval village one of the most important buildings would be the *church*. There the villagers would go to listen to the *priest* and hear the most important service, Mass. In Britain all the churches belonged to the *Roman Catholic* Church. Even the days the villagers did not have to work, known as *holy days*, were set by the Church. The priest was a very important man in his village. It was he who would *baptise* the babies, *marry* couples and *bury* the dead. He might also *teach* the local boys.

Total for exercise: 10 marks

Exercise 3.5

1. *A diocese is a grouping of churches and their priests that are controlled by a bishop.* (2 marks)

2. *A bishop is a senior churchman who controls a diocese and is based in a cathedral. In medieval times he could also be a government official and important landowner. Some, such as Odo of Bayeux, were even warriors.* (2 marks)

3. *A cathedral is a large church that is the base of a bishop in a diocese. Cathedrals were built to display the wealth and power of the bishop.* (2 marks)

4. *Tithes were taxes raised by the Church. They allowed bishops to control great wealth and live in palaces next to their cathedrals.* (2 marks)

5. *The Pope was the head of the Church, and was usually based in Rome. There could be conflict over who held the position, as the Pope controlled much wealth and had a great deal of power in Europe.* (2 marks)

Total for exercise: 10 marks

Exercise 3.6

1. *The abbot made sure his monks followed the rules by checking their beds, 'to find if they have private possessions hidden there'.* (2 marks)

2. *The writer shows that this monk is not following the rule of poverty by describing the expensive items that he owns, and claiming that he 'spared no expense': 'Greyhounds he had … fine grey fur, the finest in the land … he had a wrought-gold, cunningly-made pin'.* (3 marks)

3. This answer needs to use both sources clearly to show both sides of monastery life, referring to when the rules were kept strictly and when they were not. Pupils who also pay attention to the provenance of these sources and grasp that Source A is not an account of actual behaviour, but advice on what should be done, should be awarded top marks for this question.

    Source A shows us that the abbots were told to enforce the Rule of St. Benedict strictly. Monks would have been 'severely punished' if they were found to have private possessions. This might imply that many monks did not follow the Rule, although the source is not an account of an actual punishment but advice on what should be done. Source B could be said to confirm that some monks did not always follow the Rule. The monk Chaucer describes appears to have been too interested in hunting and fashion. However, we must remember that while he might have based his characters on real people, Chaucer was not a monk himself and his portrayal might not be accurate. (10 marks)

Total for exercise: 15 marks

Exercise 3.7

1. A full answer here will pick out the nun's education at Stratford-at-Bow and her general demeanour, and support this with an accurate quotation.

    It is clear that this nun is well-educated because Chaucer writes: 'And she spoke French fairly and elegantly/As she'd been taught at Stratford-at-Bow'. Her behaviour ('with manners, dignity and reverence') seems to reflect an educated woman. (2 marks)

2. The best answers will compare the two sources clearly and use clear, accurate quotations to point out that the nun follows the church rules far more closely.

Of the two characters portrayed by Chaucer, the nun seems to be much more interested in serving God, as is shown in the line, 'She was so charitable and full of pity'. It seems that wealth and possessions matter more to the monk: 'his sleeves were garnished at the hand/With fine grey fur, the finest in the land'. On the other hand the nun has 'manners, dignity and reverence' which suggest that she is less interested in material wealth. While the monk loves to hunt, the nun 'would weep to see/A mouse caught in a trap'. The overall impression is that the nun follows the rules of the Church much more closely than the monk. (8 marks)

Total for exercise: 10 marks

Exercise 3.8

This question would be ideal to provoke a class debate on the good and bad points of living as a monk or nun. The following table includes some examples. Pupils will have their own personal ideas and any reasonable suggestions should be accepted.

Good points	*Bad points*
Kept books, provided education	*No possessions allowed*
Helped travellers and the poor	*Gruelling schedule of services*
Tended to the sick	*Punishments*

In looking at why people wanted to join monasteries and nunneries pupils should note that ordinary life for many meant real uncertainty about food and shelter. Also, many people of the time sincerely felt the call of religion and wanted to lead 'good' lives.

Total for exercise: 10 marks

Extension questions

If the teacher wishes, there is scope here for the pupils to use their lists as the basis of an essay. Suggested questions are:

(a) Describe a day in the life of a monk or nun. (20 marks)

(b) Explain why monasteries or nunneries were important in this time period. (10 marks)

Chapter 4 From civil war to Henry II

Exercise 4.1

1. *Matilda*   (c) *was the daughter of Henry I.*

2. *William the Marshal*   (a) *was one of the great warrior knights.*

3. *Londoners*   (d) *forced Matilda to leave their city.*

4. *Stephen of Blois*   (b) *became king after Henry I.*

5. *Henry II*   (e) *was the son of Matilda.*

Total for exercise: 5 marks

Exercise 4.2

1. *Geoffrey de Mandeville changed sides when it suited him during the civil war between Stephen and Matilda, and led his soldiers on raids where they burned, stole and took prisoners. He became Earl of Essex and was killed in 1144. (2 marks)*

2. *Eleanor of Aquitaine was the heir to Poitou, Aquitaine and Gascony. She married the King of France, Louis VII, when she was thirteen, and went on the Second Crusade with him. Her marriage to Louis was later annulled and she married Henry II. She was the mother of two kings of England: Richard I and John. (2 marks)*

3. *The assizes were travelling royal courts, and part of Henry II's plan to increase royal justice. These courts took power away from the barons, helped to make a standard common law for England, and raised money for the king in fees and fines. (2 marks)*

4. *When Thomas Becket was in exile the de Broc family held his old lands. On Becket's return he claimed this land back. Some members of the family joined the four knights on their mission to kill the Archbishop in December 1170. (2 marks)*

5. *Criminous clerks were churchmen who had been accused of crimes. Originally they were tried in the Church courts, which did not punish harshly and took any fines for the Church. Henry II wanted them to be tried in the king's courts, and this dispute led to Becket's exile. (2 marks)*

Total for exercise: 10 marks

Exercise 4.3

1. The list should include most of the following reasons: *the issue of where criminous clerks should be tried; the excommunication of the king's men; churchmen leaving the country without permission; the struggle of power between crown and Church; the coronation of Prince Henry; the two powerful egos of Henry II and Becket (Henry II's temper and Becket's stubbornness).* (5 marks)

2. Pupils' lists will differ depending on the reasons to which they assign the most importance. Marks should be given for any reasonable order that can be backed up in the answer to question 3. (5 marks)

3. Pupils should be encouraged to think about how each reason might link or connect together. A class debate is often a good starting point for ideas. If this is a writing task the pupils need to start by clearly identifying what they think is the most important single reason for the argument and then show how this linked to other reasons. It would be useful to distinguish between long- and short-term factors.

   The most important reason for the quarrel between Henry II and Archbishop Becket was the struggle over power between the Church and the crown. The argument about criminous clerks, leading to the Constitutions of Clarendon in 1164, was the trigger for the two men to fight. Henry II wanted to control the Church in the way he was controlling his barons and Becket stood in his way. Both men were stubborn, with Becket having a strong belief in protecting the rights of the Church, and Henry having a quick temper. Becket saw the Constitutions of Clarendon and the coronation of Prince Henry as taking power away from the Church. Henry believed that he had authority over the Church and that he ought to be able to control the actions of churchmen. (10 marks)

   Total for exercise: 20 marks

Exercise 4.4

1. An answer should pick out two points and use quotations in doing so.

   Edward Grim describes Becket as 'the unconquered martyr' and 'this lamb' in his writing. He depicts Becket as being brave and godly by praying. (3 marks)

2. This is best answered with a comment supported by a quotation.

   Edward Grim describes one knight as 'wicked', describes his violent actions against 'this lamb' and shows the knights in a bad light by being complimentary about Becket's bravery, 'offering himself a living victim'. (2 marks)

3.   The answer should pick out the correct quotation and show an understanding of what it means.

Edward Grim writes, 'by the same blow he [the knight] wounded the arm of him who tells this', meaning that Grim himself was wounded in the attack. (2 marks)

4.   This source relates that Becket was struck four times. Pupils should use supporting evidence from the source.

Edward Grim writes that Becket was struck four times, first 'cutting off the top of the crown', then 'Becket received a second blow'. 'At the third blow he fell on his knees', and then 'the third knight inflicted a terrible wound as he lay'. (3 marks)

5.   A good answer will look clearly at Becket, Grim and the four knights when comparing the two sources. It should be clear that Grim mentions swords, while spears or lances are used in the picture, and that in the picture the knights appear to be aiming more at his body than his head (as suggested in Grim's account). There is a monk or churchmen present but he does not appear to be wounded.

The picture shows four knights attacking Becket, though two appear to have lances rather than swords as described by Edward Grim. They are also striking the Archbishop on the body rather than the head, while Grim's account tells of at least three blows to the head. The picture does show Becket with one wound to the head. The picture also shows a monk standing to the side, but he doesn't appear to be wounded and it is therefore unclear if this is supposed to be Grim. (5 marks)

Total for exercise: 15 marks

Exercise 4.5

This is a narrative essay, so chronological order will be important.

'Thomas Becket served Henry II well in government' should be followed by the information that Becket was Henry II's Royal Chancellor and also his personal friend.

Thomas Becket served Henry II well in government. Becket became the King's Royal Chancellor, and the two men were close friends.

'Henry II's mistake was to convince Becket to become Archbishop of Canterbury' should lead to how the king wanted to control the Church through Becket, how Becket reluctantly agreed to become Archbishop and then how Becket threw himself into his new role. There should be a mention of their first disagreements over the issue of criminous clerks.

Henry II's mistake was to convince Becket to become Archbishop of Canterbury. Becket did not want the job but reluctantly agreed in 1162. The Archbishop then took on his new role with enthusiasm and began to quarrel with Henry over criminous clerks. Henry wanted these churchmen to be tried in the king's courts, rather than Church courts.

'The quarrel between the two men became serious when ...' should lead to a discussion of how the issue of criminous clerks was really part of a bigger disagreement over power between the Church and the Crown. Mention should also be made of the Constitutions of Clarendon, Becket's exile at Pontigny and the coronation of Prince Henry as King of England without Becket.

The quarrel between the two men became serious when Henry tried to force Becket to agree with the Constitutions of Clarendon in 1164. These were intended to give the king much more control over churchmen. Becket refused and Henry tried to put him on trial for mishandling money while he had been Chancellor. Becket went into exile at Pontigny in France, and Henry seized his land and property. Meanwhile Henry decided to make his son, Prince Henry, the King of England so that he could devote more time to his French lands. He asked Archbishop Roger of York to conduct the coronation instead of Thomas. This caused a public outcry and the King travelled to France to meet Becket.

'Making peace in 1170 did not work' should lead to the fact that the peace did not solve the basic problem of power as Becket excommunicated the bishops and put pressure on Archbishop Roger of York. Henry II's angry outburst followed by the actions of the four knights and the de Broc family also needs to be included, leading to Becket's death at Canterbury Cathedral.

Making peace in 1170 did not work. Becket continued, in Henry's view, to misuse his powers by excommunicating all the bishops who took part in Prince Henry's coronation and complaining to the Pope about Roger of York. In a rage, Henry is said to have cried 'Will no one rid me of this turbulent priest?', which led four knights, supported by the de Broc family, to murder the Archbishop at Canterbury on 29th December 1170.

The concluding paragraph needs to look at the consequences of Becket's death. It should include how the King had to back down concerning criminous clerks and the Constitutions of Clarendon and pay penance for the murder. For the Church Becket was to become a martyr who defended its power. Pupils might be able to discover that Becket was soon made a saint and Canterbury became a shrine for him.

For Henry II, Becket's death was a disaster. He was widely blamed for the murder and had to give up his claims over criminous clerks and the Constitutions of Clarendon. In 1174 he paid penance for the murder, allowing himself to be whipped by the churchmen of Canterbury. For the Church, Becket became a martyr and a symbol of someone who stood up to interference from outsiders. A shrine to him was built at Canterbury and the Church benefited from the money brought by pilgrims.

The main narrative body of the essay should be worth 20 marks, whilst the final paragraph should be worth 10 marks. For an idea of assessing the level of understanding please refer to the marking guide in the appendix.

Total for exercise: 30 marks

Chapter 5 Richard I, the Crusades and King John

Exercise 5.1

2.   Richard rebels against his father Henry II.   (e) 1188

8.   The Pope calls for the Third Crusade.   (c) 1187

5.   Richard is crowned and decides to go on crusade.   (d) 1189

3.   Cyprus falls to Richard's soldiers.   (g) May 1191

4.   Philip II and Richard led a successful attack on Acre.   (b) July 1191

6.   The Battle of Arsuf.   (a) September 1191

1.   Richard is captured by Leopold of Austria.   (f) December 1192

7.   Richard dies attacking the castle of Châlus.   (h) 1199

Total for exercise: 8 marks

Exercise 5.2

1. Prince John was the youngest brother of Richard I. He plotted to allow King Philip of France to control Normandy, and tried to seize the English throne for himself while Richard was imprisoned. Despite this, Richard named him as his successor. (2 marks)

2. Leopold of Austria led the German crusaders to Acre but was insulted when the English threw his banner down from the city walls. In December 1192 Leopold captured Richard near Vienna and handed him over to the Emperor of Germany. (2 marks)

3. Princess Berengaria was the daughter of the King of Navarre. Despite having been engaged to the sister of King Philip for twenty years, Richard decided to marry her in 1191. (2 marks)

4. Philip II was the King of France who agreed to go on crusade with Richard I in 1191. He fell ill after the fall of Acre and returned home, where he plotted to seize Richard's lands in France. (2 marks)

5. Saladin was Richard's opponent in the Third Crusade and the leader of the Muslim forces who retook Jerusalem. His forces were defeated at Arsuf and Jaffa but he prevented Richard from taking Jerusalem. (2 marks)

Total for exercise: 10 marks

Exercise 5.3

1. The answer should show how the sources disagree on who initiated the truce and the reasons for accepting it. The inconsistency in dates should also be mentioned.

   Source A refers to 'the King of England's request for peace', which suggests that Richard asked for the truce. It also says that 'The Franks ... appeared happy and content'. On the other hand Source B says that 'When Saladin offered the same terms' as before, Richard 'could not afford another long period of haggling'. Source A makes it look like Richard asked for the peace and was happy with it, while Source B says that Saladin asked for the peace and Richard had to accept it because he was in a hurry. Source A also gives the date as 1st September, while Source B gives the 2nd. (5 marks)

2. A good answer here will attempt to look carefully at who produced each source, when it was produced, what it says and why it might have been produced. It is important that the modern historian's account is not discounted simply because it is not contemporary. A very good answer will show an understanding that a modern historian might have a fuller view of both sides in this case, whilst the author of Source A, although a contemporary and apparently an eyewitness, may only know one side. If the answer looks at one source thoroughly it should be awarded more than half marks but full credit should only be given to an answer that looks fully at both sources.

   The writer of Source A, Imad Ad-Din, is a follower of Saladin and apparently an eyewitness but would be writing from the Muslim point of view. He does give a lot of useful information, but his opinions, like 'The Franks ... appeared happy and content', are probably one-sided and written to give the impression that the terms proposed by the Muslims were fair and readily accepted by Richard. Source B is written by a modern historian, Antony Bridge, who certainly was not an eyewitness but is probably much less one-sided and would have used a number of sources. His account is factual, without much opinion, and would be useful for an overall view. Both sources are therefore useful but in different ways. (7 marks)

   Total for exercise: 12 marks

Exercise 5.4

Richard I is known as 'the Lionheart'. He was described by Richard de Templo as strong and handsome: 'graceful in figure ... his limbs were straight and flexible ... while his appearance was commanding'.

During his life he was known as a fighter. While his father, Henry II, was alive, Richard led a rebellion against him. With his brother John he defeated Henry in France and became King of England on his father's death in 1189. The Pope had called for the Third Crusade the previous year and in 1191 Richard decided to go and fight with Philip II of France against the Muslim leader, Saladin. Richard proved himself to be a strong military leader, taking Cyprus and the cities of Acre and Jaffa. Before the battle for Jerusalem, however, he negotiated with Saladin and a truce was agreed.

While in the Holy Land Richard learned that his old ally Philip of France was plotting to take his French lands. On his way home in 1192 he was captured and imprisoned by the Emperor of Germany for a ransom of 100 000 marks. Meanwhile his brother John was plotting to seize Normandy with Philip's help. Richard was released in 1194 and returned to England, crushing John's rebellion. He then spent the next four years in France fighting Philip. In 1199 Richard was killed at Châlus while attacking a castle. On his deathbed he forgave his brother John and named him as his successor.

I think that Richard I was a true hero. This is because he was an excellent fighter and commander of his army, and won several military victories. He is known as the 'Lionheart', which shows how people considered him to be brave. He captured Cyprus, Acre and Jaffa, and at home he crushed the rebellion of his brother John. He also knew when to negotiate peace rather than fight, and successfully made a truce with Saladin. However, although he was a hero, he wasn't perfect. He could be cruel and massacred thousands of Muslims in the Holy Land. He was imprisoned by the Emperor of Germany and the ransom almost bankrupted England. In spite of this, Richard's victories are what are remembered.

Total for exercise: 20 marks

Exercise 5.5

1. This is meant as a preparation exercise for the essay but 5 marks can be awarded for each list, giving a total of 10 marks.

Richard as a good king	Richard as a bad king
A great, brave warrior (capture of Acre and Jaffa)	Could not rule England effectively (only spent six months in England)
Crushed rebellion (Prince John and King Philip)	Could be cruel and ruthless (massacre of Muslims at Acre)
Supported the Church on crusade	Did not leave an heir to the throne (10 marks)

2. It is important that the writer should make an effort to explain his or her thinking and not simply copy down information. To gain full credit it is important that a clearly organised and argued conclusion is made. For further help in marking please refer to the marking scheme for part (b) of a CE essay and double the points awarded.

Looking at the evidence I think that overall Richard was not a good king.

There is no doubt that Richard was a good king in some ways. He was an excellent military leader and a brave warrior, leading his forces to capture Acre and Jaffa in the Holy Land, and he won the support of the Church by going on Crusade. He was also able to crush rebellions by his brother John and Philip II of France, and showed that he was forgiving by naming John as his successor.

On the other hand, in other ways Richard was clearly not a good king. Because he was abroad so much he was unable to rule England effectively, and this allowed his enemies to gain an advantage. He only spent six months of his ten-year reign in England. The English people were heavily taxed to pay for the Crusade and when Richard was captured in 1192 these taxes were increased to pay for his ransom. During the Crusade he could be ruthless and cruel, as is shown when he ordered the massacre of thousands of Muslims at Acre. His died because of his own carelessness, and did not leave an heir at his death, meaning that he was forced to pass the throne on to John who had proved himself untrustworthy.

In conclusion, I believe that, on balance, Richard I was not a good king. He was not a 'bad' king because he had many personal strengths. But by spending very little time in England and taxing the people heavily, he showed that he did not have the interests of the English people at heart.
(10 marks)

Total for exercise: 20 marks

Exercise 5.6

2.	*King Philip II takes Normandy from John.*	(c)	*1204*
6.	*Innocent III places England under an interdict.*	(d)	*1208*
4.	*King John is excommunicated by the Pope.*	(g)	*1209*
3.	*King John becomes a vassal of Pope Innocent III.*	(h)	*1213*
8.	*Otto IV loses the Battle of Bouvines.*	(f)	*1214*
5.	*John agrees to the Magna Carta.*	(a)	*1215*
7.	*A French army under Prince Louis invades England.*	(b)	*May 1216*
1.	*King John dies of dysentery.*	(e)	*October 1216*

Total for exercise: 8 marks

Exercise 5.7

1. As well as England, the Angevin Empire controlled more of France than the French king himself. Philip II wished to change this and set about reclaiming the French lands held by John. (2 marks)

2. Arthur was John's nephew and had a strong claim to the throne that was upheld by Philip II. John managed to capture Arthur and is reputed to have murdered him around 1203. (2 marks)

3. Scutage was a war tax that John was accused of using even when he was not at war. (2 marks)

4. The power to place an interdict was a major weapon of the Church. If an interdict was imposed it meant that church services, marriages and burials could not be held. Pope Innocent III used it against John in 1208. (2 marks)

5. Prince Louis was the son of Philip II of France. The rebel nobles declared him to be the rightful King of England and, with their support, he attempted an invasion in May 1216. (2 marks)

Total for exercise: 10 marks

Exercise 5.8

What the Magna Carta said:

Religion	Taxes	Justice
● John was not to interfere with the Church.	● John could not raise taxes without the consent of his barons. ● The level at which John could set certain feudal fees was restricted.	● Freemen could not be imprisoned or punished without a fair trial. ● Freemen could not be fined without trial and any fine should match the crime.

Total for exercise: 10 marks

Exercise 5.9

1. The best answers should use accurate quotations in support.

   According to Source A, John is good because he 'was the most resourceful of the sons of Henry II'. He was good at administration, he started national taxation and 'he brought into being the navy that thwarted King Philip's projected invasion'. (5 marks)

2. Again, a good answer will be supported by accurate quotations.

   Source B suggests that John was bad because of the cruelty he showed towards a priest named Geoffrey, who 'said it was not safe for priests to work for the King any longer'. John punished Geoffrey by imprisoning him 'in chains, clad in a cloak of lead and starved'. (5 marks)

3. A good answer here will carefully look at the provenance of each of the sources before making a clear judgment. Source A needs to be identified as by a modern historian who might have more information but would not have been alive at the time. Source B should be identified as a contemporary source by a monk, who might be repeating gossip or have a natural bias. For full credit it is essential that this answer concludes with a clear expression of which source is probably more reliable. There is no 'right' or 'wrong' answer: either source could be regarded as more reliable but there should be a cogent argument to support the claim.

   I think Source A is more reliable. This is because even though Source B is written by someone writing around the time of John, the writer is a monk who would not have been an eyewitness, picking up his information through travellers passing through the monastery. His information could be very one-sided and he may be naturally biased against John. Source A is written by a modern historian who is not so likely to be one-sided about John. The modern historian has the benefit of greater hindsight and is able to view and compare many different sources from the time. Of course, the modern historian will have no personal knowledge of events at the time but he is still probably the more reliable source. (10 marks)

   Total for exercise: 20 marks

Chapter 6 Henry III and the Edwards

Exercise 6.1

1. Henry III   (c) was nine years old in 1216.

2. Simon de Montfort   (b) won the Battle of Lewes.

3. The rebel barons   (d) forced the King to accept the Provisions of Oxford in 1258.

4. Prince Edward   (e) won the Battle of Evesham.

5. Henry III   (a) wanted his son to be King of Sicily.

Total for exercise: 5 marks

Exercise 6.2

1. The Parliament was a meeting of all the barons in a great council. The barons used Parliament to try to control the king, and Simon de Montfort tried to gain support for himself by also inviting knights and townsmen. (2 marks)

2. Prince Edward was Henry III's son whom he tried to put on the throne of Sicily. He was imprisoned with his father after the Battle of Lewes, but managed to escape and led the forces that defeated de Montfort at the Battle of Evesham. (2 marks)

3. Simon de Montfort was a powerful French baron as well as the Earl of Leicester and Henry III's brother-in law. He was the leader of the rebel barons and helped to establish the Parliament. He was killed at the Battle of Evesham in 1265. (2 marks)

4. The Provisions of Oxford formed an oath that Henry III and Prince Edward were forced to swear in 1258. The King was no longer allowed to have foreigners in government and had to do what the rebels wanted. In 1264 Louis IX of France said that the Provisions were not valid. (2 marks)

5. The Battle of Evesham took place in 1265 between Prince Edward on one side and Simon de Montfort on the other. Prince Edward rescued his father, and de Montfort and his closest associates were killed. (2 marks)

Total for exercise: 10 marks

Exercise 6.3

1. *A good commander and warrior – Henry III was defeated and imprisoned at the Battle of Lewes, and had to be rescued at the Battle of Evesham by his son, Prince Edward. He repeated the mistakes of his father King John about exercising control over his barons.* (2 marks)

2. *Supporter and protector of the Church – Henry III had Westminster Abbey rebuilt and promised to go on crusade. However, the Pope threatened to excommunicate him after the failed attempt to make Prince Edward King of Sicily.* (2 marks)

3. *Just and fair – Henry III used outsiders and foreigners to run his government. There is a suggestion that he might have had Richard Marshall killed. He did agree to the Magna Carta, even though he did not always agree about what it meant.* (2 marks)

4. *He left a son to rule after him – Henry III left Prince Edward, an experienced soldier, as the heir to the throne.* (2 marks)

Total for exercise: 8 marks

Exercise 6.4

1. A good answer to this question will state the answer in the pupil's own words, then support this with a quotation.

    When the battle started Henry III ran away from Simon de Montfort: 'As soon as the King saw Edward, he withdrew himself'. (2 marks)

2. Again, a good answer will first state the information in the pupil's own words, then support this with a quotation.

    Other than Simon de Montfort, the other people killed included his son Henry and Hugh Despenser: 'Simon de Montfort, Earl of Leicester, his son Henry and Hugh Despenser, were among the many who were slain'. (2 marks)

3. A good answer here will clearly pick out that the author of Waverley Annals thought highly of Simon de Montfort and perhaps not so highly of Henry III, though the writer's opinion of the King is only implicit.

    The writer of the source makes it clear that he thinks highly of Simon de Montfort by describing him as 'that most worthy knight'. He also implies that the King ran away and played no part in the fighting. It is therefore likely that the author has more sympathy with de Montfort than with the King. (4 marks)

Total for exercise: 8 marks

Exercise 6.5

Edward I was crowned in *1272*. Unlike his father, *Henry III* he did not have many problems and was happy to use Parliament to pass *statutes*. He was very harsh to the *Jews*, whom he drove out of the country. Edward was forced by his nobles to agree that *Parliament* had to agree to any attempts to raise *taxes*.

Total for exercise: 6 marks

Exercise 6.6

1.

1.	Anglesey	(d)
2.	Berwick	(c)
3.	Falkirk	(b)
4.	Snowdonia	(e)
5.	Stirling Castle	(a) (5 marks)

2.

1. *Anglesey provided Llewelyn and his forces with food, so in both campaigns Edward seized the island. He built Beaumaris Castle there.* (2 marks)

2. *Berwick was an important border town that Edward took in 1296 when he defeated John Baliol.* (2 marks)

3. *Falkirk is where William Wallace and his army were defeated by the English at a battle in 1298.* (2 marks)

4. *Snowdonia is the mountainous area where Llewelyn based himself in order to prevent any invasion by the English.* (2 marks)

5. *Stirling Castle was the last Scottish castle holding out against the English. When it fell in 1304 Edward was in command of Scotland.* (2 marks)

Total for exercise: 15 marks

Exercise 6.7

1. *Edward had the dream of uniting the British Isles under his control. He believed that Prince Llewelyn wanted to create a single Welsh princedom and had too much power and influence in Wales. Between 1274 and 1276 Llewelyn continually refused to pay homage to the King. Edward attacked in 1276, using three armies to cut Llewelyn off from his food supplies in Anglesey. Llewelyn was forced to surrender. When war broke out again in 1282 Edward again cut the Welsh off from Anglesey. He then built castles to protect his position and forced the Welsh to accept English laws and officers. (10 marks)*

2. *In 1292 Edward had chosen John Baliol as King of Scotland. However, he continued to interfere in Baliol's decisions. In 1295 the Scottish made an alliance with France, which Edward saw as a betrayal. He seized control of Berwick and deposed Baliol. However, Edward found it difficult to hold on to Scotland because of men like William Wallace and Robert Bruce, who resisted English control. Wallace defeated the English at the Battle of Stirling Bridge in 1297 but was himself defeated at Falkirk the following year. He was eventually captured and executed in 1305. In 1306 Robert Bruce started to lead the Scottish resistance and conduct raids into England. Edward died in 1307 while preparing to lead the English army into Scotland once more. (10 marks)*

3. *Edward understood that he needed to rule the country correctly and according to the law. He realised that he needed Parliament to raise taxes, and began to use Parliament to pass statutes, which became the most important laws of the land. An example was the Statute of Gloucester which gave more power to the royal courts than the barons' courts. However, some things Edward tried to pass alone. The Statute of Mortmain attempted to restrict the amount of land that went to the Church. He also drove all Jews out of England and confiscated their property. The money raised from this, and the taxes agreed to by Parliament, helped to finance Edward's continuing wars with the Welsh, Scots and French. (10 marks)*

Total for exercise: 30 marks

Exercise 6.8

1. *Source A states that any Jews who remained in England after 1st November would 'be beheaded'. (2 marks)*

2. *Source B tells us that King Edward did a number of things in memory of his wife. He 'offered unceasing prayers on her behalf' and 'gave generous grants of alms and celebrations of Mass for her'. He also ordered that crosses be built in her memory 'in every place where her funeral carriage had rested'. (3 marks)*

3. This answer should clearly list at least three terms, which could include:

   'flower of Christendom', 'handsome and great', 'powerful in arms', 'he had no equal', 'vigour and valour'. (3 marks)

4. A good answer will clearly compare Source C with both other sources. It should be made clear that Source B shows a grief-stricken Edward who shows generosity, whereas Source A shows Edward's ruthless nature. A final statement will conclude that, in providing evidence of Edward's character Source A disagrees with Source C the most.

   Source C is full of praise for Edward, calling him 'the flower of Christendom'. The general impression is that he was a kind, brave and gentle man. It appears to agree with the description given in Source B, which describes Edward's reaction to his wife's death: 'For the rest of his days he mourned for her … He gave generous grants of alms and celebrations of Mass for her in various places around the kingdom'. On the other hand, Source A describes Edward's actions in expelling the Jews from England, showing him to be a ruthless and cruel king: 'an edict went out from the King ... no Jews should remain in the land upon pain of death'. Source A therefore does not agree with Source C as much as Source B does. (7 marks)

   Total for exercise: 15 marks

Exercise 6.9

1. *Piers Gaveston was a knight from Gascony and was Edward II's favourite. He was exiled and then executed by the Earl of Lancaster's men. (2 marks)*

2. *Thomas, Earl of Lancaster was a powerful English noble who wished to influence the King. He was responsible for the execution of Piers Gaveston and seized control after the Battle of Bannockburn. However, in 1321 he was beheaded as a traitor. (2 marks)*

3. *Robert Bruce (the younger) claimed the Scottish throne and attempted to drive the English out of Scotland. His attacks on Stirling Castle in 1314 led to the Battle of Bannockburn, in which he defeated the English. (2 marks)*

4. *The Statute of York was passed in 1322. It declared that a king's subjects could not attack his royal power and restricted the power of Parliament. (2 marks)*

5. *The Despensers were royal favourites of Edward II and they used this position to take lands. When Queen Isabella led a revolt against Edward II, both Despensers (father and son) were executed. (2 marks)*

   Total for exercise: 10 marks

Exercise 6.10

1. The list of Edward II's failures could include the following main points:

   - *He failed at warfare (Battle of Bannockburn);*
   - *He relied heavily on his favourites (Gaveston, the Despensers);*
   - *He argued with his nobles, causing them to rebel (Lancaster);*
   - *He failed to keep his wife Queen Isabella happy and loyal. (5 marks)*

2. There is no agreed order in which the reasons may be placed. What is important is that the pupil makes clear and cogent comments about why one reason is more important than the others. An example follows:

   - *He argued with his nobles, causing them to rebel.*
   - *He failed at warfare.*
   - *He relied heavily on his favourites.*
   - *He failed to keep his wife Queen Isabella happy and loyal.*

   The most important reason why Edward II failed as a king was because he failed to work with his nobles. A king cannot rule properly without the support of most of his nobles and Edward angered them by being a poor military commander and having favourites. When Queen Isabella rebelled against him, Edward found that the nobles were unwilling to support him. (10 marks)

   Total for exercise: 15 marks

Exercise 6.11

Edward III became king after his mother *Queen Isabella* and her lover *Roger Mortimer* seized power from *Edward II*. After taking control, Edward had to deal with problems on his northern border with *Scotland*. He was also having problems with the King of France over control of *Gascony*. This helped lead to the outbreak of the *Hundred Years'* War. Edward III had some successes against the French king, including the naval battle at *Sluys* and at the Battle of *Crécy*. The war was halted when the *Black Death* struck both France and England.

At the end of his reign, however, the *Good Parliament* in 1376 showed that not every Englishman was happy. Because the *Black Prince* had also died, Edward III's death meant that nine-year-old *Richard II* was to be the next king.

Total for exercise: 12 marks

Exercise 6.12

1. *Philip VI of France had taken the throne of France instead of Edward III. He attacked Edward's holdings in France, but his forces lost the Battles of Sluys and Crécy. (2 marks)*

2. *The Battle of Sluys was fought on the 24th June 1340. The English, led by Edward III, attacked the French fleet and the French fleet, unable to manoeuvre because it was in three lines, was defeated. (2 marks)*

3. *The Siege of Calais happened after the English victory at the Battle of Crécy. The town was defended by Jean de Vienne and held out for months until Philip VI abandoned it in July 1347. Edward III ordered that six burghers should be beheaded but Queen Philippa persuaded him to spare them. (2 marks)*

4. *The Battle of Poitiers was fought on the 19th September 1356. The English nobles wished to keep fighting in France in order to gain more lands for themselves. The Black Prince fought a larger French army and won, capturing the King of France, John II. (2 marks)*

5. *The Good Parliament was held in 1376. Edward III needed money raised from taxes, but the Commons refused until he accepted a number of reforms, including the removal of his bad advisors. However, the King's son John of Gaunt managed to reverse many of the reforms within a year. (2 marks)*

Total for exercise: 10 marks

Exercise 6.13

1. A good answer will state what happened and then use a quotation to support this.

   Source A states that the crossbowmen were killed by the French men-at-arms, who were impatient at the crossbowmen's lack of success against the English: 'the French men-at-arms rode down the crossbowmen'. (2 marks)

2. This answer should pick out several things that the crossbowmen did and support this with quotations from the source.

   Source B states that when the Genoese crossbowmen were fired upon they tried to run away and threw away their crossbows. The source says 'some of them cut the strings of their crossbows, others flung them to the ground, and all turned about and retreated'. (3 marks)

3. A full answer should clearly describe the scene in the picture and compare this with Sources A and B, showing that it does show men-at-arms charging but does not show crossbowmen.

Source C shows the battle with soldiers fighting each other on foot and men-at-arms charging each other. In this respect it agrees with both Sources A and B, as A says the French 'charged headlong forward' and Source B states that the horsemen 'drove upon the Genoese'. On the other hand the picture does not show the crossbowmen at all, and therefore it does not support the description of the bowmen's actions in Sources A and B. What it does show is a cannon in the foreground and several cannon balls and, in the background near the windmill, some form of machine is being used to hurl rocks. (7 marks)

4. A good answer here will attempt to look at the provenance of each source as well as its content in trying to make a judgement. Pupils should point out that Source A was written by someone who had talked to an English knight who was at the battle, whilst the author of Source B was not an eyewitness but again spoke to people at the battle and was working for Edward III's wife. All we know about Source C is that it was produced in the century after the battle.

   Of the three sources, two give useful information about the Genoese crossbowmen. Source C is probably the least useful as it does not show the crossbowmen at all and was produced in the next century after the battle, so is unlikely to have been by an eyewitness. Sources A and B, however, both give information about how the crossbowmen were killed by the French. Both of these sources are based on information from eyewitnesses, with Source A based on an account from a knight who was there. He would probably give the English view. Jean Froissart, who wrote Source B, travelled a lot and spoke to many people, so he might have picked up information from both sides and certainly his account has much more detail. So probably Source B is the most useful to a historian, although Source A also has useful information. (8 marks)

   Total for exercise: 20 marks

Chapter 7 Life in the Middle Ages

Exercise 7.1

1.   *A motte was a man-made hill that was part of an earth and timber castle ('motte and bailey'), first built in England by the Normans. The tower on the top of the motte was the final refuge for the inhabitants when the castle was attacked. (2 marks)*

2.   *Curtain walls were stone walls surrounding a castle, often replacing the earlier wooden palisade fence. They were usually constructed around shell keeps or tower keeps. (2 marks)*

3.   *The portcullis was used to close off the entrance to a castle by dropping down over the doorway from above. (2 marks)*

4.   *Murder holes were set in the ceiling of a castle entrance to allow defenders to drop stones and hot liquids on attackers. They also allowed the castle's defenders to put out fires set against the entrance doors by dropping water on the flames. (2 marks)*

5.   *A barbican was an outer gatehouse set before the main gate to provide extra protection. (2 marks)*

Total for exercise: 10 marks

Exercise 7.2

The chart could include any of the following:

Advantages	Disadvantages
A secure place to live	*Not built for comfort*
Included a chapel	*No privacy for less important people*
Own water source	*Obvious target for attack or siege*
Plentiful supplies of food	
Comfortable rooms with privacy for important people	

Total for exercise: 10 marks

Exercise 7.3

1. *John besieged the castle using rock throwing machines and arrows, and sending knights to attack. He then used miners to undermine the outer walls and the keep walls.* (3 marks)

2. *This source does not mention King John using siege towers or battering rams at the siege of Rochester.* (2 marks)

3. A good answer to this question needs to concentrate on the tactic of besieging the castle. John's use of miners should be referred to as the successful method of taking the castle, though an answer concentrating solely on the use of undermining should not earn full marks.

   The castle finally fell because its defenders ran out of food. The source says 'not a morsel of provisions remaining amongst them, the besieged ... surrendered'. In order to bring the siege to a conclusion, John had used miners to bring down the castle walls and force the besieged people into the keep. Clearly, the most successful method of taking Rochester Castle was undermining. Other methods such as hurling stones and throwing missiles proved less effective than the miners who 'threw down a great part of the walls'. (5 marks)

4. This answer should use clear quotations from the source to show that Roger of Wendover was sympathetic to the rebel barons.

   The writer of this source does not seem to like King John much, as he states that the rebels 'feared greatly the cruelty of the King'. He describes the defenders as having 'great bravery and boldness', and praises their honour when he writes that, 'thinking it would be a disgrace to die of hunger when they could not be conquered in battle, [they] surrendered'. The impression given is that the writer is sympathetic towards the rebel barons. (5 marks)

   Total for exercise: 15 marks

Exercise 7.4

1. *Usury was the crime of charging interest for a loan of money. This was something that the Catholic Church did not allow, and is why the Jews were seen as useful as they were not bound by this rule.* (2 marks)

2. *Pogroms were deliberate anti-Jewish attacks. They occurred in York in 1190 and London in 1264.* (2 marks)

3. *Propaganda is information that is deliberately one-sided in order to influence people, such as the blood libel used against the Jews.* (2 marks)

4. *Blood libel refers to false stories that were spread about the Jewish people. For example, they accused Jews of killing Christian children.* (2 marks)

5. *The Medici family was an Italian family that defied the Church's rulings about usury in the later Middle Ages.* (2 marks)

Total for exercise: 10 marks

Exercise 7.5

1. This answer should point out that there are several places where Chaucer shows the dislike of the Jews, and quote them.

    Source A shows how the Christians disliked the Jews in line 5: 'Hateful to Christ, and hated by Christians'. The reasons why they were hated were for their 'foul usury and shameful profits' (line 4). Chaucer also uses the term 'cursed Jew', which shows the narrator's dislike of the Jews. Indeed, if we consider it to have been written from a Christian point of view, the whole story shows the Christian attitude towards Jews, who appear violent and bloodthirsty in this story of the murder of an innocent boy. (5 marks)

2. Some guidance will be needed to elicit a full answer to this question. One approach could be to ask pupils first to explain how this story has no value to a historian as the story is likely to be at best an exaggeration, at worst a total fabrication. Then ask what the source does actually tell us about feelings and beliefs during the time of Geoffrey Chaucer. Does this make the source useful to historians?

    This story is false propaganda and probably does not describe a true event. Therefore it cannot be used to support the claim that Jews killed Christian children. However, the fact that it is a piece of propaganda is useful in understanding how the Jews were viewed in Chaucer's time. Stories like this would have been widely known and believed, and this gives us an idea as to how Jews were persecuted. (5 marks)

Total for exercise: 10 marks

Exercise 7.6

1. *By saying 'I have never seen it with the outer eyes of the flesh', Hildegard is saying that she has never actually seen her visions except inside her own head.* (3 marks)

2. *The source shows that Hildegard did not consider herself to be equal to men because she writes, 'more than wretched in being a woman' and describes herself as an 'unworthy maidservant' and 'servant-girl'.* (5 marks)

Total for exercise: 8 marks

Exercise 7.7

1. Pupils should choose an aspect of medieval society (the nobility, farming, the Church, etc.) and give ways which support and deny the notion that the role of women was regarded as important. The example used below concerns women in the nobility.

   The role women played in the nobility was significant in some ways but very limited in others.

   In some ways the role women played in the nobility was very important. Kings and nobles needed a wife to produce an heir and ensure the continuation of their line. Often marriages were arranged when the boy and girl were still children and would include an agreement as to how lands would be divided up between the two families. Kings often married foreign women to ensure friendly relations with, or to extend their rule over, another country. In the case of Eleanor of Aquitaine, a noble woman could also be an important figure whom the public supported and, as the wife or mother of a king, could also be a political tool.

   In other ways women's roles were limited because many people did not believe they could hold positions of authority. Despite being named by Henry I as his successor, Matilda could not hold on to the throne of England because she did not have the support of the barons, churchmen, or people. Women like Eleanor of Aquitaine were very much the exception: usually they were expected to keep away from public affairs and simply produce children for their husband.

   In conclusion, the role women played in the nobility was clearly important, but so limited that they could never enjoy equal status with men. (20 marks)

2. A good answer will be categorised and look at a few different elements of medieval society. The sample answer below assesses the opportunities available to women in the Church, society in general, and in authority.

   There are a number of reasons why there were not as many opportunities for women as for men in the medieval period. These included the role of the Church, the legal position of women, and the idea of what made a good ruler.

   Women were not given a very equal chance in the Church because churchmen regarded woman as secondary figures. They looked at the Bible and argued that because Christ's disciples were men, women should not be allowed to hold positions of authority (except within nunneries). Women were not allowed to preach, so when the new orders of friars were introduced to take advantage of the Church's wealth, women were left behind and still had to live like nuns.

   The legal position of women was not very strong because they were not allowed to hold property. In a marriage, the husband held the land on behalf of his family. Before the Magna Carta, widows were forced to remarry if they wanted to retain their lands. Women were normally prevented by the guilds from entering trades, though they were supported as the wives of members.

Women had little chance to rule because of the beliefs of the time. Most nobles did not regard women as effective leaders and would have resented being led by a woman themselves. This is a major reason why Matilda was unable to hold on to the throne of England and why the nobles supported Stephen instead.

Women certainly had some opportunities to show their ability in the medieval period, such as in nunneries, running a craft or trade in a town or aiding their husbands. However, it is clear that because of a lack of opportunities given to them, medieval women were not given an equal chance with men in the medieval world. (20 marks)

Total for exercise: 40 marks

Exercise 7.8

In the medieval world doctors depended upon the work of ancient *Greek* and *Roman* doctors such as *Galen*. Surgery was the job of the *barber-surgeon*. Sickness was blamed on *bad air*, the *position of the planets* or *God's punishment*.

The Black Death came from *Asia*. It had two forms, *bubonic* and *pneumonic*. The first major European city to suffer was *Florence* in the country of *Italy*. It reached England in *1348*, first infecting the port town of *Melcombe* in *Dorset*.

Total for exercise: 16 marks

Exercise 7.9

The cartoon or the paragraph should include the following key points: the fleas feed on an infected rat; the bacteria multiply in the flea's stomach; the starving flea tries to feed on a human and passes on the bacteria. For full marks the pupil should have found out that the name of the bacteria that caused the Black Death was *Yersinia pestis*.

Total for exercise: 5 marks

Exercise 7.10

1. *The symptoms of Bubonic Plague included the appearance of buboes, sickness, dark blotches, great pain (from the nervous system being attacked) and death within five days. (2 marks)*

2. *The symptoms of Pneumonic Plague included fever, bleeding on the lungs and death within two days. (2 marks)*

3. *In order to avoid the plague medieval people prayed to God, cleaned up the towns, stayed clear of the sick and tried to filter bad smells with flowers or herbs. (2 marks)*

4. *In order to cure the plague medieval people cut open buboes or used frogs to try and soak up the poison. (2 marks)*

5. *Flagellants were religious people who believed that, if they whipped themselves, they would pay penance for others' sins and God would stop the plague. (2 marks)*

Total for exercise: 10 marks

Exercise 7.11

1. *The people of Florence took a number of different steps to stop the plague from coming. They were involved in 'the cleansing of the city from many impurities', they refused 'entrance to all sick folk', and made 'humble prayers addressed to God'. (3 marks)*

2. *The people of Florence tried a number of different ways to deal with the plague. Some wanted to 'shun and abhor all contact with the sick' whilst others decided 'to drink freely ... to take their pleasure with song and revel'. (2 marks)*

3. *Giovanni Boccaccio was a man living in Florence when the plague struck in 1347 and was thus an eyewitness. He wrote down what he had actually seen and experienced. This source is therefore likely to have accurate information about how the people in Florence reacted to the plague. However, it can only tell us about the people's reaction in Florence rather than the rest of Europe. (5 marks)*

Total for exercise: 10 marks

Exercise 7.12

1. *The men of Gloucester would not let other people into the town, they 'refused those of Bristol entrance to their country'. (2 marks)*

2. *According to Geoffrey, people believed that the plague was spread by 'the breath of those who lived amongst people who died of the plague'. (2 marks)*

3. *Both these sources show how people at the time tried to keep outsiders away. Boccaccio wrote of 'the refusal of entrance to all sick folk', while Baker told of how the men of Gloucester 'refused those of Bristol entrance to their country'. However, Boccaccio also wrote about other measures such as 'humble prayer', 'the cleansing of the city' and the use of 'flowers or fragrant herbs' which are not mentioned at all by Baker. (4 marks)*

Total for exercise: 8 marks

Exercise 7.13

This answer should give an account of the spread of the plague in Britain and the manner in which the people tried to deal with it, both through prevention and cure. A conclusion should assess how effective these solutions were.

> The Black Death was a disaster for the people of Britain when it arrived from Europe. It first came in June 1348, when two ships carrying the disease arrived at the town of Melcombe in Dorset. Soon it had reached the major ports of Southampton and Bristol, and spread inland from there.
>
> The people of medieval Britain had a number of different beliefs about what was the cause of the Black Death. It was believed that the air was unclean, or that the dirt in the streets was the cause, or contact with the sick. Followers of the Church believed that the disease was God's punishment for the people's sins.
>
> There were all sorts of ideas of how to deal with the Black Death, either by preventing it or curing it when caught. Some thought that cleaning the streets and using perfumes to clear the air would help. Those who believed that it was a punishment from God prayed constantly, and a group of people called flagellants appeared, claiming that they could pay penance for people's sins by whipping themselves. For the unfortunates who had caught the plague, doctors tried cutting the buboes open, or using frogs to absorb the poison.
>
> None of the solutions offered to cure or prevent the spread of the plague worked, and the survivors had to wait until 1350 for the disease to die out of its own accord. The failure of the flagellants meant that people lost respect for the Church, and some villages were abandoned because so many of the villagers died.

Total for exercise: 20 marks

Exercise 7.14

1. The points could be arranged as follows.

Good Things	Bad Things
Better pay and working conditions	High death toll
Growth of colleges	Raised prices for craftsmen's work
More opportunities for women	Towns and monasteries struggled
English language used much more	Women had to work harder
Smaller population meant more food available later	Villages abandoned

Many of the points mentioned could arguably be placed in either column. Give credit for points well explained in either list, even if there is some overlap, and encourage a class discussion on how best to categorise them. (10 marks)

2. This answer should give both the good and bad consequences of the Black Death, and end with an assessment of which of the consequences was the most significant for England.

The Black Death resulted in many changes in medieval England. Many people suffered greatly, while others benefited. When the plague was over, England had changed both for the better and worse.

The most obvious consequence of the Black Death was the high death toll. It is estimated that one third of England's population died between 1348 and 1349. Whole towns and villages were wiped out and cities were halved in size. Enclosed orders of monks and nuns were particularly at risk and struggled to survive. There became a shortage of craftsmen and workers, meaning that prices rose dramatically. Women had to work harder to make up for the lack of men.

On the other hand, the Black Death did bring benefits to some people. The lack of workers meant better pay and working conditions for those who survived. Because so many churchmen had died, not many people could now speak Latin and instead, English became the language of teaching. Colleges were founded to educate more scholars. There were also more opportunities for women in business to take over from the men who had died.

Clearly, the Black Death changed England. However, the most important consequence of the plague was the change in society. The population was always able to grow again but now people had more opportunities in work and education, and better living conditions. This brought along several problems as well. The Statute of Labourers forced peasants to accept the wages they had had before the Black Death. Dissatisfaction caused by this was to play a part in the coming of the Peasants' Revolt in 1381. (20 marks)

Total for exercise: 30 marks

Chapter 8 Richard II and life in the towns

Exercise 8.1

5.	Poll Tax is introduced.	(i) 1377
9.	The rebels enter London.	(g) 13th June 1381
4.	Sudbury and de Hales are killed.	(f) 14th June 1381
1.	Wat Tyler is killed at Smithfield.	(d) 15th June 1381
3.	The Merciless Parliament is called.	(e) 1388
8.	The Lords Appellant hand power back to Richard.	(j) 1389
10.	The Lords Appellant are arrested.	(a) 1397
2.	Death of John of Gaunt.	(c) February 1399
7.	King Richard II is deposed by Parliament.	(h) September 1399
6.	Richard II is murdered.	(b) February 1400

Total for exercise: 10 marks

Exercise 8.2

1. The Poll Tax was used to pay for the war in France. It was used in 1377, 1379 and 1381, when everyone over the age of fourteen had to pay a shilling. (2 marks)

2. John of Gaunt was Richard II's uncle. He ruled in place of Richard when the King was still a child. On his death in 1399, John's lands were seized by Richard, which started the events that led to his being deposed. (2 marks)

3. Wat Tyler was one of the leaders of the Peasants' Revolt and came from Kent. He met with the King at Smithfield in June 1381 and was killed there. (2 marks)

4. The Merciless Parliament was a response to Richard's rule in 1388. It demanded the arrest and trial of Richard's officials, leading to the death of Sir Simon Burley. (2 marks)

5. The Lords Appellant were a group of nobles made up of the Duke of Gloucester and the Earls of Arundel, Warwick, Nottingham and Derby. They ruled for a year after the Merciless Parliament. (2 marks)

Total for exercise: 10 marks

Exercise 8.3

1. *The source states that Wat Tyler struck out at the Mayor of London when the Mayor tried to arrest him: 'Tyler struck the Mayor in the stomach with his dagger'.* (2 marks)

2. The answer to this question will depend heavily on how the pupil interprets the picture on page 125. Most have determined that Tyler is the figure in red, with the mayor represented by the figure in blue raising his sword above Tyler's head. However, it can be argued that the mayor is actually the red horseman, about to draw his sword in defence of the attack by Tyler (in blue). Neither interpretation allows the picture to be entirely reconciled with the account of the *Anonimalle Chronicle* but, depending on which they choose, pupils will find different things in common.

   If the first interpretation is used (Mayor in blue, Tyler in red), then the picture agrees with the *Chronicle* in that the Mayor strikes Tyler (with the position of the sword suggesting a neck or head wound), though the picture does not suggest that it was done in retaliation. If the second interpretation is used (Tyler in blue, Mayor in red), then it can be argued that the picture is showing an earlier stage of the account given by the *Chronicle*, in which Tyler attempts to attack the Mayor, who draws his sword in defence. (6 marks)

Total for exercise: 8 marks

Exercise 8.4

Good points	Bad points
Dealt with Peasants' Revolt successfully	*Very young when becoming king*
Truce with France	*War with France went badly*
Had strong control over the country	*Allowed officials to be executed in 1388*
Created a personal army	*Introduced Poll Tax*
	Murder of political opponents (1397)
	Did not keep his word to the peasants
	Seizing of John of Gaunt's lands (10 marks)

If this is to be answered as an essay, then it could be broken down into an introduction, two content paragraphs and a conclusion.

Did Richard II deserve to be deposed? There are a number of reasons for and against the action taken by Parliament in 1399.

On the one hand, Richard II did not deserve to be deposed. He had dealt with the Peasants' Revolt successfully, with little change for the nobility. Since this event he maintained a strong control of the country, with little rebellion. He also succeeded in negotiating a truce with France, halting the war that had been going badly since the end of the reign of Edward III, and which had caused much unhappiness amongst the peasants.

On the other hand, there are reasons why Richard II did deserve to be deposed. He may have dealt with the Revolt, but in doing so he did not keep his word to the peasants. Instead, he continually used force to suppress any further rebellion. In 1397 he arrested two of the Lords Appellant, having two killed and one exiled. On the death of John of Gaunt in 1399, he unlawfully seized the lands which should have been inherited by Gaunt's son Henry Bolingbroke. This was the spark that led to Bolingbroke's revolt and Richard's downfall.

I believe that Richard II did deserve to be deposed. His good points were usually tainted by a bad action. He may have stopped the Peasants' Revolt but he did so dishonestly. He kept order in England but did so by murdering his opponents. (20 marks)

Total for exercise: 30 marks

Exercise 8.5

(a) The 'describe' section of this question should include the entry into London, the meeting at Mile End, the murders of Archbishop Sudbury and de Hales, the meeting at Smithfield and details about Tyler's death.

Wat Tyler was a leader of the rebels who led the peasants into London to demand their rights from Richard II. The villeins were unhappy about not being paid wages and argued that nobody should be bound to their lord. Others were paid a small amount but wanted more. There was also unhappiness about the war in France (which had been going badly), and certain priests, such as John Ball, began to stir up resentment towards the Church. The Revolt was finally triggered by the Poll Tax which, in 1381, forced everyone over the age of fourteen to pay a shilling. Most peasants found this impossible to pay, and sparked the uprising at Brentwood in Essex.

Wat Tyler was from Kent and came to prominence as a leader of the rebels. The men of Kent and Essex attacked government officials such as tax collectors, and some were killed. Tyler led the men of Kent to London in June 1381, where prisons were broken open and buildings were set on fire. On the 14th June, the King met the rebels at Smithfield and agreed to the majority of their demands. However some, including Tyler, were not satisfied. The Archbishop of Canterbury and the King's Treasurer were both dragged from the Tower of London and executed.

When Richard met the rebels again at Smithfield on the 15th June, Wat Tyler presented himself as their leader. He demanded that all lordships should be abolished except for the king, and for all Church lands to be seized. The Anonimalle Chronicle claims that after calling for water, Tyler 'rinsed his mouth in a very rude and disgusting fashion before the King. Then he made them bring him a jar of ale, of which he drank a very great deal.' When a gentleman described him as 'the greatest thief and robber in all Kent', Tyler tried to kill him and was arrested by the Mayor of London. When he tried to attack the Mayor, a fight broke out in which Tyler was killed by one of the King's men. (20 marks)

(b) As this is the analytical or 'explain' part of the essay, a description will not do here. Pupils need to break down the reasons here into categories, such as the use of armed force and severe punishments, lack of leadership following the death of Tyler, and the trust of the rebels in the king's promises.

Richard II was able to defeat the rebels during the Peasants' Revolt for a number of reasons. First, he had the support of his nobles who could use military force to fight the peasants. Richard met the rebels at Mile End and Smithfield accompanied by a force of his own men, who were able to protect him and use force to put down the rebellion. Once it had ended, rebel leaders like John Ball were caught and hanged. Secondly, the peasants lacked effective leadership. Wat Tyler was persuasive but his character led to his being killed. With his death, the peasants were without a leader at all and they dispersed. Thirdly, Richard used persuasive arguments that they should remain loyal, and was willing to reason with the people face-to-face. He initially agreed to their demands, which caused most of the peasants to leave, making it easier to put down any rebellion that remained. (10 marks)

Total for exercise: 30 marks

Exercise 8.6

1.	*Most town houses*	(b)	*were made of wattle and daub.*
2.	*Some of the worst smells in a town*	(c)	*were made by butchers.*
3.	*Boys who were trained in a trade*	(e)	*were known as apprentices.*
4.	*Charters*	(d)	*were legal documents allowing town government.*
5.	*Some important buildings like churches*	(a)	*were made of stone.*
6.	*When the 'hue and cry' was raised, everyone had to*	(g)	*chase the criminal.*
7.	*One thing a guild did was to*	(f)	*provide mystery plays.*

Total for exercise: 7 marks

Exercise 8.7

1. *While most people worked in the country, towns grew slowly in the medieval period and new towns were also built. They were often on major roads or river crossings.* (2 marks)

2. *Guilds were organisations founded to protect and organise their craftsmen members, and also played a role in town government. They had their own rules and supported their members if they were in difficulty.* (2 marks)

3. *Apprentices were boys being trained in a craft through an indenture with the master craftsman. Apprenticeships lasted seven years or more, after which the apprentices became journeymen. They were often involved in trouble in town because they went around in large groups enjoying themselves.* (2 marks)

4. *Since towns had large numbers of people in them, crime was inevitable. Cut-purses, or pickpockets, and other petty criminals operated in towns so keys and locks were developed. When a criminal was discovered, the 'hue and cry' was raised and people had to help chase after him.* (2 marks)

5. *In crowded towns, the disposal of rubbish and waste was a constant problem. It led to outbreaks of diseases such as the Bubonic Plague, and death was so common that towns relied on newcomers to keep their populations stable* (2 marks).

Total for exercise: 10 marks

Exercise 8.8

The picture or the paragraph needs to make clear the crowded and dirty nature of the medieval streets. The street should also be busy, showing some of the businesses and crafts to be found in a town. Different types of people should be shown, possibly including beggars and apprentice boys. Smells could include both rubbish and the result of manufacturing. Sounds could include the noises of various crafts and the regular chimes of church bells.

Total for exercise: 10 marks

Exercise 8.9

1. *The baker is being publicly humiliated by being dragged on a sledge with a loaf of bread (probably the one he tried to cheat a customer with) around his neck.* (3 marks)

2. A good answer will note that in all three cases the guilty party is punished by being publicly humiliated. It should also be made clear that the extract about John Penrose is different in that Penrose has wine poured over him, whilst the other two sources concern bakers who are made to carry their bad loaves around their necks. For full credit pupils must back these statements up with clear quotations from the extracts.

    The picture agrees with the sources since in all three cases the dishonest trader is being publicly humiliated. John Penrose had wine 'poured over his head', and Robert Porter was 'put in the pillory' with some bread around his neck. The picture also shows a baker being humiliated with a loaf around his neck.

    However, a part of John Penrose's punishment is that he can no longer work as a vintner unless he is pardoned. There is no reference in the picture as to whether the baker is given a similar punishment. Also, Robert Porter is put in the pillory for his punishment, whereas the baker in the picture is being dragged through the streets instead.

    Overall, the picture agrees in some ways with the written sources but not about every detail. (7 marks)

Total for exercise: 10 marks

Chapter 9 The three Henrys

Exercise 9.1

Henry IV became King in *1399* by overthrowing King *Richard II*. Because of the way he had become King, *Henry IV* had problems holding on to his crown. The Welsh under *Owain Glyndwr* rebelled, while to the north the *Scots* were causing problems. In 1403 the *Percy* family rose in revolt, but Henry '*Hotspur*' was defeated at the Battle of *Shrewsbury*.

Henry IV also had money problems and *Parliament* forced him to allow councillors to control his finances. At his death the matter of how the *Lancastrian* kings had obtained the throne was to cause problems in the years ahead.

Total for exercise: 10 marks

Exercise 9.2

Traditionally, an obituary should be a positive record of the deceased's life but pupils should be encouraged to provide a balanced view of their subject. This essay may be mostly narrative but must contain an analytical element.

> *Henry IV was the son of Edward III's third son John of Gaunt, and so had a claim to the throne. He was a Lord Appellant who initially supported Richard II but the King's distrust of him caused Henry to be sent into exile. On the death of John of Gaunt in February 1399, Richard seized Henry's inheritance, causing him to return to England. He won the support of the most important nobles and arrested Richard, who was deposed in September 1399. Henry was then named King by the nobles, despite the Earl of March having a better claim, being descended from Edward III's second son Lionel.*
>
> *Henry IV had to deal with a number of problems, such as the rebellion by Welsh leader Owain Glyndwr, who proclaimed himself the true Prince of Wales and seized many of the English castles there. In 1403 the Percy family tried to place the Earl of March on the throne and allied with Glyndwr but Henry defeated them at the Battle of Shrewsbury. With Henry distracted by trouble at home, the French attempted to take Gascony and Calais. Henry was able to defeat all these threats successfully, but this cost money and he proved himself poor at controlling what he spent. However, he was willing to work with Parliament, and the royal councillors they provided remained loyal and were able to help with his duties.*

In conclusion, Henry IV can be regarded as a successful king. He left England, Wales and Scotland far more stable than they had been under Richard II, and had managed to solve the succession question with the Earl of March. However, the manner in which he took the crown was to cause problems in later years.

Total for exercise: 20 marks

Exercise 9.3

1. The English were so successful in France because they

2. The Burgundians were important to Henry V because they

3. Henry V is best known because he

4. The greatest success the English had was when they

5. By the Treaty of Troyes, Henry V

(d) faced the French while they were divided by civil war.

(a) allied with the English.

(e) won the Battle of Agincourt.

(b) took control of Normandy.

(c) became next in line to the French throne after the death of Charles VI.

Total for exercise: 5 marks

Exercise 9.4

1. *Owain Glyndwr was the leader of the Welsh rebels fighting against Henry IV. He made an alliance with the Percy family but this failed and the rebellion was crushed. (2 marks)*

2. *The Lollards were members of a religious movement that was founded by John Wycliffe. They believed that the Bible needed to be in English, and some even questioned the power of the Pope. (2 marks)*

3. *Charles VI was the mentally ill King of France whose forces lost to Henry V in Normandy. He was forced by the Treaty of Troyes to accept Henry V as the heir to the French throne. (2 marks)*

4. *The Duke of Burgundy was the leader of the Burgundians. His murder by the Armagnacs led to the new Duke, Philip, allying himself with the English and helping to agree to the Treaty of Troyes. (2 marks)*

5. *The English and Burgundians forced King Charles VI of France to agree to the Treaty of Troyes in 1420. Under the treaty, Henry V married Catherine of Valois and was made the heir to the French throne. (2 marks)*

Total for exercise: 10 marks

Exercise 9.5

1. This answer should use a quotation from the source to show that the prisoners were killed because of the fear of a new French attack.

   According to Source A, the prisoners were killed because the English believed that the French were about to attack from the rear. The source states, 'This was to prevent them [the prisoners] turning on us in the fighting that was about to happen'. (2 marks)

2. A good answer here will point out the differences in the opinions of 'the monk of St. Denis' and Ghillebert de Lannoy. However the best answers will note that neither opinion can really be said to *disagree* with Source A, since Source A only reflects the writer's belief of an imminent attack, and is not an assertion that the attack actually happened (and that the killing of the prisoners was therefore necessary). It is possible to reconcile all the sources.

   Source B gives the opinions of two chroniclers. A 'monk of St. Denis' claimed that in fact the French did not intend to attack, and that the killing of the prisoners was 'based on a panicked response to a false alarm'. Ghillebert de Lannoy claims that Antoine, Duke of Brabant, rallied his troops and that this prompted the order to kill the prisoners. However, both opinions could possibly agree with Source A, because Source A only talks about 'a shout' that went up about a possible attack. The monk of St. Denis claims that this was a false alarm whereas Ghillebert de Lannoy claims that the Duke of Brabant caused it. (6 marks)

3. This answer needs to look at the provenance of each source and make a judgement based on this.

   Both sources are useful for understanding the event. The Gesta Henrici Quinti was written at the time by someone who was probably with Henry's army and might have been an eyewitness. It therefore gives a first-hand account of the battle from the English perspective. Source B is by a modern historian who was not at Agincourt. However, it summarises the opinions of two other contemporary writers and gives a more balanced view than could have been held by the author of the Gesta Henrici Quinti at that time. (7 marks)

   Total for exercise: 15 marks

Exercise 9.6

Henry V won an unexpected victory at the Battle of Agincourt. It is important to know how and why this happened.

The campaign that led to the battle began at Harfleur in August 1415, with the English intending to march on a chevauchée north to Calais. Henry wanted to take advantage of the civil war in France between the Armagnacs and the Burgundians in order to reclaim land from the French. However, both sides allied to fight the English and blocked the River Somme with their troops. The English were forced to march east until they found a place to cross and continue north but their path was blocked once again on the evening of the 24th October, in a field outside the town of Agincourt.

The exact figures are still debated but it is clear that the English were heavily outnumbered by the French. Some have said that there were ten times as many French as there were English. The English had little food and were forced to sleep outside in the rain. Some accounts claim that, in desperation, Henry attempted to strike a deal with the French, offering to pay for damages and return Harfleur to them if they would be allowed to get to Calais.

The battle itself began in the afternoon of the 25th October. The English were divided into three 'battles', commanded by Lord Camoys, the King and the Duke of York. Groups of archers were placed in the gaps between each battle. During the morning they planted stakes in front of them and waited for the French charge. However, the French were waiting for reinforcements and did not intend to attack. Finally, the English advanced to within 300 yards of the French, planted their stakes again and fired their arrows. The French cavalry attempted to charge the English archers but the field had turned muddy with rain and conditions were difficult. The narrowness of the battlefield forced the French closer together and their plate armour made it difficult to move. The second line advanced but was held up by the sheer number of bodies lying in the mud. Any French nobles who were captured were held for ransom, though a belief that the French were attacking from the rear led Henry to order that the prisoners be killed. Seeing what had happened to the rest of their army, the third French line rode away.

In the end, the reasons Henry V won the battle included his superior tactics, the mistakes made by the French, and Henry's good luck. Henry did well to contain the French forces into a narrow area where they could not move effectively. His archers were encouraged to fight hand-to-hand when their arrows were used up, and the English footsoldiers were well trained and equipped. Meanwhile, the French were disorganised and their cavalry were unable to charge effectively in the mud. They were also waiting to receive reinforcements when the English advanced.

Total for exercise: 20 marks

Exercise 9.7

2.	Henry VI becomes King of England.	(h)	1422
10.	English forces are defeated at Orleans.	(g)	1428
3.	Joan of Arc is burnt at the stake.	(i)	30th May 1431
9.	Henry VI marries Margaret of Anjou.	(c)	1449
7.	Jack Cade's rebellion.	(j)	1450
6.	Henry VI suffers a mental collapse.	(e)	Summer 1453
4.	Henry VI's son Edward is born.	(a)	October 1453
5.	Richard, Duke of York, becomes protector.	(f)	March 1454
8.	Henry VI recovers from mental illness.	(b)	1455
1.	Somerset is killed at the Battle of St. Albans.	(d)	22nd May 1455

Total for exercise: 10 marks

Exercise 9.8

1. Richard, Duke of York was next in line to the throne after Henry VI, until the King had a son in 1453. He was regent while Henry VI was ill and seized control of the King after the Battle of St. Albans. (2 marks)

2. Jack Cade led a Kentish rebellion in 1450. On entering London, he failed to control his rebels and was hunted down and killed. (2 marks)

3. Edmund Beaufort was the Duke of Somerset and a rival to Richard of York. He fell from power during Henry's illness but regained it when the King recovered. He was killed at the Battle of St. Albans in 1455. (2 marks)

4. The Battle of St. Albans was fought between Yorkists and Lancastrians on 22nd May 1455. The Yorkists feared that the Lancastrians were planning to arrest their leaders. When the Yorkists fought their way into St. Albans, a number of Lancastrian leaders were killed, including Somerset, and Henry VI was captured. (2 marks)

5. Queen Margaret was the daughter of the Duke of Anjou and married to Henry VI. She took more control as the King became ill and was a key leader of the Lancastrians, becoming a determined enemy of Richard of York. (2 marks)

Total for exercise: 10 marks

Exercise 9.9

The following sample answer uses the example of Henry IV.

I have chosen Henry IV because I admire the way he stood up for his rights and overcame his enemies.

Henry IV was the son of John of Gaunt, the third son of Edward III. He was perceived as being a threat to Richard II and was exiled. When the King seized his inheritance on the death of John of Gaunt in February 1399, Henry returned from exile, gained the support of the nobles, and deposed Richard. He was named as his successor and ruled for fourteen years.

Probably the most important things that happened during the reign of Henry IV were his taking of the throne, the defeat of the rebels opposed to him, and the introduction of royal councillors by Parliament. In taking the throne from Richard II, Henry cleared up the succession issue (for the time being at least). The young Earl of March had a stronger claim, being the grandson of Edward III's second son Lionel, Duke of Clarence. However, when an attempt was made by the Percy family to replace Henry with the Earl of March, the King defeated them at the Battle of Shrewsbury in 1403. There was also a Welsh rebellion by Owain Glyndwr, who claimed to be the true Prince of Wales, but this too was defeated. Henry worked well with Parliament but proved poor at controlling how he spent his money. Parliament forced him to accept royal councillors who were able to control his finances for him, which they did effectively.

In conclusion, Henry IV is important in the history of his country because of the stability he brought after the reign of Richard II. He defeated rebellion by those opposed to his rule and started a new dynasty of kings that eventually led to the Tudors. His reign also saw changes, such as the use of royal councillors, that made government more effective.

Total for exercise: 20 marks

Chapter 10 The Wars of the Roses

Exercise 10.1

1. The Lancastrians — (b) outnumbered the Yorkists during the Wars of the Roses.

2. The Act of Accord — (d) stated that Richard of York was to be king after Henry VI.

3. Richard, Duke of York — (c) was killed at the Battle of Wakefield in 1460.

4. The Battle of Towton — (e) was the bloodiest battle of the Wars of the Roses.

5. Richard Neville — (f) fought for both sides in the Wars of the Roses.

6. Prince Edward — (a) was killed at the Battle of Tewkesbury in 1471.

7. Henry VI — (h) was murdered in the Tower of London.

8. The Earl of Warwick — (g) was killed in the Battle of Barnet in 1471.

Total for exercise: 8 marks

Exercise 10.2

1. Queen Margaret was the wife of Henry VI. During his illness Margaret sought to defend the King's position and that of her son against the challenge of Richard of York and his son Edward IV. (2 marks)

2. Elizabeth Woodville was married to Edward IV. The marriage was unpopular with Edward's principal advisor, the Earl of Warwick, and this helped to turn Warwick against the Woodville family. Elizabeth was the mother of the 'Princes in the Tower', Edward and Richard. (2 marks)

3. The Earl of Warwick was Richard Neville, a nephew of Richard of York. He was known as the 'Kingmaker', due to the fact that his support for the King was considered essential to his holding on to the throne. He first backed Edward IV, then changed sides to support Henry VI, and died at the Battle of Barnet. (2 marks)

4. Richard, Duke of Gloucester was the brother of Edward IV. He supported the King, was rewarded and became very powerful. (2 marks)

5. George, Duke of Clarence was another brother of Edward IV but was not very trustworthy, having joined Warwick to oust Edward, only to rejoin Edward. He was later executed for treason in 1478, some say by being drowned in a barrel of Malmsey wine. (2 marks)

Total for exercise: 10 marks

Exercise 10.3

2.	Edward IV dies.	(d)	April 1483
6.	Richard seizes the throne.	(f)	July 1483
5.	The execution of the Duke of Buckingham.	(c)	November 1483
4.	The Battle of Bosworth.	(b)	22nd August 1485
1.	The Battle of Stoke	(g)	16th June 1487
7.	Perkin Warbeck attempts to invade England.	(a)	1495
3.	The execution of Perkin Warbeck.	(h)	23rd November 1499
8.	The execution of Edward, Earl of Warwick.	(e)	28th November 1499

Total for exercise: 8 marks

Exercise 10.4

1. Margaret of Burgundy was the sister of Edward IV. She was an enemy of Henry VII and she supported both Lambert Simnel and Perkin Warbeck. (2 marks)

2. Lambert Simnel was a young man who pretended to be Edward, Earl of Warwick. Supported by the Earl of Lincoln, he sailed from Ireland and was defeated by Henry's forces at the Battle of Stoke. Henry VII eventually gave him a job in his kitchens. (2 marks)

3. The Earl of Lincoln supported Lambert Simnel's claims. He led the army that landed in England and fought Henry VII at the Battle of Stoke, where he was defeated and killed. (2 marks)

4. The Battle of Stoke was fought near Newark on the 16th June 1487. Henry VII's forces defeated the Earl of Lincoln and his army. The King felt secure enough on his throne after the battle to have Elizabeth of York crowned Queen. (2 marks)

5. The Earl of Warwick had a strong claim to the throne of England, being the nephew of Edward IV and Richard III. He was kept locked up in the Tower by Henry VII and was executed on 28th November 1499 as a result of Simnel's and Warbeck's failed rebellions. (2 marks)

Total for exercise: 10 marks

Exercise 10.5

1. This answer needs to point out that the 'Princes in the Tower' were a danger to Richard III as they had a better claim to the throne than he had.

   Richard III wanted the two boys killed 'because as long as they lived he could never be out of danger'. As the sons of Edward IV, they had a stronger claim to the throne. (2 marks)

2. The correct answer will name the two murderers (according to More) but should also mention Sir James Tyrell.

   According to Sir Thomas More, the actual murderers of the two princes were Miles Forest and John Dighton. They were appointed by Sir James Tyrell. (3 marks)

3. This answer needs to clearly pick out the agreement about the involvement of Tyrell and the disagreement about the way the princes died.

   Both Polydore Vergil and Sir Thomas More agree that Richard chose Sir James Tyrell to carry out the murders. Vergil states 'he committed the charge of hastening the slaughter unto James Tyrell'. More says that 'Sir James Tyrell devised that they should be murdered in their bed'. However, Vergil and More do not agree about the way that the princes died. Vergil writes that 'with what kind of death these children were executed is not certainly known', while More states the murderers 'suddenly lapped them up among the clothes, and so bewrapped them and entangled them' until the boys were dead. (7 marks)

4. A good answer here will need to look clearly and fully at both sources and make a substantiated judgement on each.

   When examining how trustworthy these sources are it is important to look at their background. Neither Polydore Vergil nor Sir Thomas More was an eyewitness to the events. Both were encouraged to write by Tudor monarchs who had reason to blacken Richard III's name. It is clear that More's source of information about the two princes is not very trustworthy, as there is no record of Sir James Tyrell confessing to the murders. Vergil would have only had the rumours of the time on which to base his claims. Therefore, neither source can be said to be entirely trustworthy concerning the deaths of the two princes. (8 marks)

   Total for exercise: 20 marks

Exercise 10.6

This narrative essay should follow the standard form of brief introduction, content and a clear conclusion. Extra marks could be awarded for pupils who not only tell the story, but can also show links between ideas and events and can point out key points or moments.

The Battle of Bosworth was an important moment in English history as it marked the beginning of Tudor rule. Yet it could easily have turned out differently.

Some people questioned Richard III's right to the throne. It was rumoured that he had ordered the heirs to Edward IV, the 'Princes in the Tower', to be killed. The King was already unpopular, having been ruthless in executing his opponents such as Lord Hastings, a supporter of Edward IV. The House of York may have had the throne but the Wars of the Roses were not over. There remained Henry Tudor, a descendant of Edward III who was exiled in France. He landed in August 1485 and his army met Richard's outside Market Bosworth in Leicestershire.

At the beginning of the battle the two sides were not very evenly matched. Richard's army easily outnumbered Henry's, and he had a superior position at the top of Ambion Hill. However, Richard was unable to trust his commanders, especially the Earl of Northumberland. Also another force, led by Sir William Stanley and his brother Lord Thomas, caused uncertainty. William was married to Henry Tudor's mother but Richard was holding Thomas's son as a hostage. It was therefore unclear which side their 3000 troops would join.

The battle began when the Lancastrian forces (led by the Earl of Oxford) engaged the front division of the Yorkists (led by the Duke of Norfolk). Richard watched from the top of the hill but, seeing Henry's banner left vulnerable, decided to charge straight at him. Seeing Richard and his entourage break ranks, the Stanleys decided to defend Henry and attacked Richard's troops. Meanwhile, the soldiers commanded by Northumberland stayed where they were. Richard was killed and his army fled.

It is claimed that Richard's crown was found on the battlefield and Lord Stanley placed it upon Henry's head. He was now King of England and the Tudor dynasty had begun.

Total for exercise: 15 marks

Exercise 10.7

This should be a fuller essay than Exercise 10.6 in that it should have both narrative and explanatory sections.

Richard III took the throne of England in 1483. He faced distrust and rebellion before losing his life at the Battle of Bosworth in 1485.

The unexpected death of Edward IV led to Richard's coming to the throne. At first, however, it was not at all clear that he would become king. Edward's true heir was his son Prince Edward. However, he was still a child, so Richard decided to place him and his younger brother in the Tower of London, supposedly to protect them against enemies. In reality, Edward's widow's family, the Woodvilles, also wanted to control the young prince and Richard wanted to stop them. However, when Edward was to be crowned in July 1483, Richard declared the boys illegitimate and took the throne for himself. Soon afterwards, the boys disappeared.

The new king had a number of problems to face and he was not totally successful in the way he tried to solve them. It was rumoured that he had ordered the 'Princes in the Tower' to be killed, and this had already made him unpopular, especially in the south where he did not have as much land or influence. The Duke of Buckingham rebelled against him and, though Richard managed to crush it, the rebellion showed that even his supporters were growing dissatisfied.

Richard's reign came to an end with his defeat at the Battle of Bosworth. Despite his army outnumbering Henry Tudor's, he did not have the full support of his commanders and could not count on the troops led by the Stanley family to join his side. While he fought bravely, his conduct in battle was poor and he was reckless in charging towards Henry with only the support of his immediate entourage.

Richard had a very short time to show if he was a good or poor king. On the one hand, he was successful because he was generally supported in the north, and was ruthless in putting down his enemies such as the Woodvilles and the Duke of Buckingham. On the other hand, Richard was a poor king because he could not gain the full support of either his people or his nobles. He was strongly suspected of having had the 'Princes in the Tower' killed, and the manner in which he had seized the throne led to many wanting him replaced by Henry Tudor.

Total for exercise: 30 marks

Exercise 10.8

Henry VII became King of England in 1485 at the Battle of Bosworth. During his reign he always managed to stay one step ahead of his enemies until, by 1500, he was secure on his throne.

When Henry VII took the crown he faced a number of problems. He had only a weak claim to the throne, being descended from an illegitimate daughter of John of Gaunt. He married Elizabeth, the daughter of Edward IV, to try to gain Yorkist support. The most powerful remaining Yorkist was Margaret of Burgundy, the sister of Edward IV. She masterminded the claim of Lambert Simnel, a young man who pretended to be the Earl of Warwick, a possible Yorkist claimant to the throne. He had the support of the Earl of Lincoln and a battle was fought with Henry's men at Stoke on 16th June 1487. Henry won, the Earl of Lincoln was killed, and Simnel was sent to work in Henry's kitchens.

The most dangerous attempt to overthrow Henry was made in 1491. A man named Perkin Warbeck was persuaded by Yorkists to pretend to be Richard, Duke of York, the younger of the two 'Princes in the Tower'. With the support of Margaret of Burgundy, an invasion of England was plotted. Henry's spies found out about this, and that Sir William Stanley was involved. Stanley was executed, and an attempted invasion was defeated in 1495. Warbeck and his supporters then went to Scotland where they made an alliance with the Scots. When Henry defeated them, Warbeck went to the West Country where he was defeated once more and captured. He was executed in November 1499 along with another Yorkist claimant, the Earl of Warwick.

In the end, Henry VII was successful in solving the problems he faced when he became king. This was because he had strong support and a good political mind, and his opponents' plots were flawed and disorganised.

Total for exercise: 30 marks

Appendix

Essay questions: generic mark scheme. Total: 30 marks

Selective description

e.g. Describe the key features of… etc.

Mark	Target	Causation / recall of knowledge
1-8	Level 1	Simple statements offering some features / ideas supported by some knowledge; embryonic, inaccurate or irrelevant knowledge; lacking real coherence and structure.
9-15	Level 2	More developed statements giving features supported by more relevant knowledge; thinly substantiated passages; uncertain overall structure.
16-20	Level 3	Developed selection of features with sound substantiation and structure; good range of features; for top of level, answer will show clear linkage and relevant importance of features.

Evaluation / Analysis

e.g. Explain why…

Mark	Target	Evaluation of factors against one another / definitions of success and failure / contextual assessment
1-4	Level 1	Simple statement offering basic and largely unfocused opinion.
5-8	Level 2	More developed analysis with some coherent judgement; some substantiation of assertions.
9-10	Level 3	Precisely selected knowledge in a clear framework of argument; strong and developed analysis / assessment with cogent judgements; strong substantiation of assertions.

Evidence questions: mark scheme. Total: 25 marks

Mark	Target	Comprehension of source
1	Level 1	Incomplete or imprecise answer.
2	Level 2	Answer which more clearly substantiates from the source.

Mark	Target	Comprehension of source
1	Level 1	Incomplete or imprecise answer.
2–3	Level 2	More developed understanding.

Mark	Target	Corroboration by cross-referencing sources
1	Level 1	Simple statement which makes a basic comment on a source.
2–4	Level 2	Answer which is more developed, connecting Source C to another source with a substantiated argument.
5–6	Level 3	Fully-developed answer which examines all three sources using a substantiated argument.

Mark	Target	Evaluation of sources for utility / consideration of provenance
1–2	Level 1	Simple statement which makes a basic comment on a source, looking only at the content.
3–5	Level 2	Answer which recognises that different sources can be useful for different purposes. For lower reaches of this band, relies on generalised comments, such as 'it depends on what you want to know' or 'all sources are useful in one way or another'.
6	Level 3	Developed and substantiated analysis of all three sources, looking at both content and provenance, and contextual appreciation that they all, in their own way, help our understanding of the argument.

Mark	Target	Making a judgement about an interpretation, relating analysis of sources to contextual knowledge
1–3	Level 1	Answer which makes little or no use of sources or makes little or no use of own knowledge. There is poor argument, little or no substantiation and only vague / embryonic statement of agreement / disagreement.
4–6	Level 2	More developed answer, making better use of sources in terms of content and with some own knowledge *or* good use of own knowledge but weaker use of sources.

7–8 **Level 3** Answer which makes full and intelligent use of all three sources, examining content and interleaving answer with accurate and pertinent own knowledge. For top of this level, the candidate will have written a very cogent and well-structured answer, with judicious appreciation of the sources and own knowledge in equal measure.

 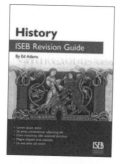  

Also available from Galore Park

English
Junior English 1
Junior English 1 Answers
Junior English 2
Junior English 2 Answers
Junior English 3
Junior English 3 Answers
So you really want to learn English 1
So you really want to learn English 1 Answers
So you really want to learn English 2
So you really want to learn English 2 Answers
So you really want to learn English 3
So you really want to learn English 3 Answers
English Practice Exercises 11+
English Practice Exercises 11+ Answers
English Practice Exercises 13+
English Practice Exercises 13+ Answers
English ISEB Revision Guide

Mathematics
Junior Maths 1
Junior Maths 1 Answers
Junior Maths 1 Teacher's Resource
Junior Maths 2
Junior Maths 2 Answers
Junior Maths 2 Teacher's Resource
Junior Maths 3
Junior Maths 3 Answers
So you really want to learn Maths 1
So you really want to learn Maths 1 Answers
So you really want to learn Maths 1 Worksheets
So you really want to learn Maths 2
So you really want to learn Maths 2 Answers
So you really want to learn Maths 2 Worksheets
So you really want to learn Maths 3
So you really want to learn Maths 3 Answers
So you really want to learn Maths 3 Worksheets
Mathematics Questions at 11+ Book A
Mathematics Questions at 11+ Book A Answer Book
Mathematics Questions at 11+ Book B
Mathematics Questions at 11+ Book B Answer Book
Mixed Maths Exercises Year 6 Pupil Book
Mixed Maths Exercises Year 6 Answers
Mixed Maths Exercises Year 7 Pupil Book
Mixed Maths Exercises Year 7 Answers
Mixed Maths Exercises Year 8 (Lower) Pupil Book
Mixed Maths Exercises Year 8 (Lower) Answers
Mixed Maths Exercises Year 8 (Upper) Pupil Book
Mixed Maths Exercises Year 8 (Upper) Answers
Mathematics ISEB Revision Guide
Mathematics Pocket Notes

Science
Junior Science 1
Junior Science 1 Answers
Junior Science 1 Teacher's Resource
Junior Science 2
Junior Science 2 Answers
Junior Science 2 Teacher's Resource
Junior Science 3
Junior Science 3 Answers
So you really want to learn Science 1
So you really want to learn Science 1 Answers
So you really want to learn Science 1
    Teacher's Resource
So you really want to learn Science 2
So you really want to learn Science 2 Answers
So you really want to learn Science 2
    Teacher's Resource
Science Pocket Notes – Living Things
Science Pocket Notes – Materials and Their
    Properties
Science Pocket Notes – Physical Processes

Geography
So you really want to learn Geography 1
So you really want to learn Geography 1 Answers
So you really want to learn Geography 2
So you really want to learn Geography 2 Answers
Geography ISEB Revision Guide
Revision Crosswords for Common Entrance and
    Scholarship Geography

History
Junior History 1
Junior History 1 Answers
Junior History 2
Junior History 2 Answers
Junior History 3
Junior History 3 Answers
So you really want to learn History 1
So you really want to learn History 1 Answers
So you really want to learn History 2
So you really want to learn History 2 Answers

Religious Studies
Religious Studies for Today
Bible Stories for Today
Religious Studies ISEB Revision
Preparing for Common Entrance Religious Studies